Arctic Adventure

Arctic Adventure

Arctic Adventure

Manfred Zepf

Arctic Adventure

Around the World Publishing LLC
4914 Cooper Road Suite 144
Cincinnati, Ohio 45242-9998

This book recounts the true experience of the Manfredo Zepf,
as translated and edited by Ron Mueller.
Personal names of participants are fictitious.

An Arctic Adventure by Manfred Zepf: Copyright © March 2019

All rights reserved,
including the right of reproduction,
in whole or in part in any form.

ISBN 13:978-1-68223-167-8

Distributed by Ingram
Cover Picture by:Natures Moment SUK - Shutterstock
Cover Design by: Ron Mueller

Dedication:
I dedicate this book to,
Ana Rita, my wife that I love the most.
Helga, daughter that I love the most.
Flávio, son that I love the most.
I love each the most and only have one of each!

My posthumous tribute to:
A great friend,
A great hunter,
A great adventurer
Above all,
A great Man of character and family.
God Bless you, Bill,
wherever you are.
Rest in peace!

Table of Content

Introduction	1
Diary Day 1: Destination the Arctic Circle	5
Diary Day 2: Arrival at "Manfred" Lake	21
Diary Day 3: The Paradise from the Hand of God	33
Diary Day 4: Moose Meat and Two Bears	41
Diary Day 5: Cabin Logs and Northern Lights	53
Diary Day 6: Destructive Visitors	61
Diary Day 7: A cold and Moose-less day	75
Diary Day 8: Partridges and a Moose	81
Diary Day 9: A Bonfire of Beauty and Emotion	89
Diary Day 10: Of Tripods and Pulleys	99
Diary Day 11: World of Super Reality	103
Diary Day 12: Good Memories and Cowboy songs	111
Diary Day 13: An Absence of Guests and the Hoot of an Owl	117
Diary Day 14: A Waterfall from the Sky	121
Diary Day 15 Two Bears and a Ridge Pole	125
Diary Day 16: The Rice Pot and the Squirrels	129
Diary Day 17: A Dream of Legend	133
Diary Day 18: Tranquility	137
Diary Day 19: Bears, Storm and Missing Canoe	141
Diary Day 20: Fantastic Paddle and Wonderful Sleep	149
Diary Day 21: Mama, Papa and Baby Bear	153
Diary Day 22: The Bear Proof Door	159
Diary Day 23: A Monster, the Paddle, Hungry Visitor	165
Diary Day 24: Marvelous Culinary Event and Mosquitoes	171
Diary Day 25: The Immensity of Peace	175
Diary Day 26: Roof Tiles	181
Diary Day 27: Honey, Chocolate and Caramel	183

Diary Day 28: Northern Light Ballet, the Dance of the Bears   187

Diary Day 29: A Floor, A Hammock, and Reading Comfort   193.

Diary Day 30: Drink of the Gods   197

Diary Day 31: No Bill!   205

Diary Day 32: God Save Canada   211

Epilogue   215

About Manfredo Zepf   225

About the Translator/Editor   227

Appendix 1,   228

Appendix 2   229

Appendix 3   229

Introduction

This is a work based on true facts, extracted from my diary, which was meant to record my feelings at the time and not the emotions of a dream, or an adventure, it was recorded without pretense of great achievements or the future. It was my attempt without any pretension other than to be able to remember the wonderful moments that I experienced.

Today I would not undertake such an adventure. And I would not recommend it to people, in general. To venture in this way, it is necessary to; develop your knowledge and techniques of hunting; to study about bears; to have the ability to instinctively handle a rifle as if it were the extension of your hand, your arm. After constant practice it becomes instinctive and automatic. I do not need to think, I do not need to look to lock or unlock or to load and eject a round from my Weatherby 30-06 Vanguard rifle.

Arctic Adventure

It is especially necessary to study and know about bear habits and habitats. You will never know exactly what is going on in the bears' head and what will be their reactions. In fact, it is of no use other than to have a general understanding of their instincts and actions. There is nothing mathematical or linear about the actions of the "Ursus Horribilis", the bear. It is a beast for which we do not have a scientific book that gives us full knowledge of its habits.

I studied a lot before making the decision to make this trip. I went when I was single. I would not have gone if I had been married. I would not have gone for the love I have for my wife Ana Rita, and my children Helga and Flávio.

Today I know that I could leave a widow and orphans, because you will see in the telling of the story that the danger was incessant, and that luck was my companion.

For reasons of rights, I have excluded the original names of people who were part of this adventure, except for my dear brother Conrado, a gift that God placed beside me in preparation for this journey. This brother who did not participate in this adventure with his presence but was constantly present in my thoughts and situations of this adventure.

My friend and fanatic, hallucinating, inveterate hunter Lairton also was not part of this adventure. He was a born hunter, who would fit into any age of history on this planet, where the horse was still the best way to get around. He himself says that these " jockey clubs" that are under the hoods of this modern world no longer match and do not make the grade.

To all those who became an integral part of this adventure, my tender thanks, and an eternal remembrance of each one of you!

Encourage those who fit wisely and knowingly into any type of adventure.

Do, because if no one else ventures, the electrifying passages and life experiences will end. It would be a sad end to miss the real adventures and live only in the virtual and the unreal ones.

Manfredo Zepf

Manfred Zepf

Diary Day 1:

Destination the Arctic Circle

December is a hellish heat here in Brazil and it is snowing on the top side of the world. So, my contact with Bill on the telephone, with the marked climatic contrast was a source of envy for both of us. He wanted to be here under the scorching tropical sun, and I wanted the cold at the border of the Arctic where the outdoor temperature was a minus eight degrees centigrade,

It was the first phone call with Bill to set the date for my future trip to act on my dream to build a hunting lodge on the Arctic border.

I met Bill years ago when Conrado, Lairton, Rui, and I went for a hunt in the same Canadian province. Horst a guide, who would take us to this hunt, met Bill, his friend and seaplane pilot, by chance at our boarding gate where we all stayed together. Horst told us that if we wanted to schedule future adventures, he recommended Bill. He introduced Bill as a professional and an excellent guide.

Arctic Adventure

Bill wasted no time in distributing his card to us and did a speedy advertisement of his services. He showed his expertise using a book with enlarged photos of places where he took groups to camp on the edge of fishing lakes and where there was abundant hunting.

To get ready for my dream adventure, I made countless contacts with Bill to make sure that all the necessary arrangements for this adventure were made.

Meanwhile I took care of the other preparations and arrangements to be made in Brazil.

This would be a unique trip that I would do on my own. Nothing could be forgotten. Some items, if forgotten, could prove to be fatal.

Four preparation months passed, until finally April came. It came along with the anxiety of packing for a challenging adventure trip. I was excited. It was hard for me to sleep.

As the traditional suitcases would not withstand the challenging conditions of the air transport that the luggage would face, I had two bags made with reinforced truck canvas and had two heavy duty boxes made to carry tools and groceries.

Then, I started packing.

I picked up my checklist for hunting trips. I had it ready so that nothing would be forgotten. The list was developed from having suffered when I forgot some critical item. In hunting trips when you forget something you can be sure you will suffer.

The rather long detailed checklist list is in the appendix. It is long and is divided into two columns with space to tick off when the item is in the suitcase. I used this list on previous trips to Africa, Canada and to the Arctic.

Despite being in Canada, this trip was very different from the other Canadian trips. I would be alone in the middle of nowhere close to the Arctic Circle and the polar cap. This would be in a place where it would be fatal to forget certain items.

It would be hundreds of miles from the nearest tiny bit of civilization.

Many of the items on the list are not known by newer, younger generations.

Despite a not-so-distant experience some curious items are on the list.

Some twenty, thirty, or forty years of technical progress has transformed all previous electronics into artifacts and museum pieces. Newer versions of them are on the list, also the clothes have improved. Some examples are mitten heaters, under the foot liners that release friction induced heat when walking, ski glasses, waterproof matches, use of a wooden clasp to attach a flashlight to the barrel of the rifle, use of graphite grease for camcorders, thermal protector for camcorders, ammunition, and batteries.

I have, like every hunter, a place at home, where I keep all my hunting equipment. In my case, it is a cramped closet that holds all my hunting equipment in an organized mess. It is a closet that I need to open carefully lest what is in it falls out on top of me.

I separated the clothes that had been stored for almost a year and needed to be washed. There were thin-insulated camouflage trousers and coats for moderate cold, zero to minus fifteen degrees Fahrenheit. There was a cold-resistant sleeping bag good to minus five degrees Fahrenheit. The heavy-duty stuff I hung out in the sun.

All the rest of the clothes got a good washing. They were also put in the sun. These clothes are always thicker than the usual ones by being in the sun they lose the scent of the soap. This keeps the bear, that is endowed with nearly forty times the smelling power of a dog, from smelling the hunter.

My plan was to take only what was strictly necessary to prevent suffering on my part. I did not spare on the cold clothes that I had once acquired to face a harsh Arctic winter hunt. That time when I went hunting for the musk ox was the time when I faced a negative thirty-five degrees Fahrenheit. This was the lowest temperature in my life.

In places like the Arctic, you do not get many second chances. In case of any surprise or disaster, you need to be well prepared. The preparation gives you have a better chance at surviving.

The Arctic experience I had two years before was of inestimable importance. I learned about the Arctic habitat and it also lit the fuse for this trip.

Arctic Adventure

That experience with Loshi, an authentic Inuit Eskimo who was my hunting guide then and who, even with his broken English, was an excellent teacher and passed on his experiences of a life that I would summarize in two words: survival and adventures!

Yes, living in adverse weather conditions such as those in the Northwest Territories one of the wildest places on the planet, where the entire province has no more than 53,000 inhabitants, and its capital, Yellowknife, is populated with only 12,000 fixed dwellers, adventure becomes part of daily life, it leaves no space for the mistakes.

With his life experience, with his knowledge of survival and love of the Arctic, like any other animal, Loshy was 100% integrated in the environment. To get an idea of his weather resistance, Loshy was able to ride on his swift Siberian husky dog sled, with no glasses and his tears didn't freeze. However, I could not bear more than a breeze that quickly froze my tears.

What struck me about him was his instinct, yes, his instinct was paranormal. He could see the storm coming as if he was a weather station, and in the endless plains, without reference due to the gray of the sky and the endless expanse of snow he always knew the compass direction. A phenomenon that I can only accept as a survival instinct.

He taught me how to handle bear attacks, how to protect the food, how to handle hunting and how to handle being hunted, how to fish, and finally he added: "Not all those that respect and love the Arctic survive, only the Arctic survives.

So much for remembering and applying previous experiences.

Finally, the travel bags were complete but not stuffed. They had a mission to endure the "tender and delicate" treatment of those who deal with baggage, and then they would have to settle into a seaplane with reduced capacity.

Nothing could be missing. From gloves to binoculars, from waterproof matches to candles, they all had to be available when needed. Each item had its quantity duly calculated, with the prudence of having the essentials, and a certain reserve.

After fitting my trusty Weatherby 30-06 rifle into an appropriate "case", there were two additional boxes that would complete the baggage. These boxes were made of light pine and reinforced with steel angles that I used in "cases" to transport sound equipment and light for my company. These angles would make the boxes more resistant to this trip. They would make a one-way trip. They had to resist the "delicate" handling of the airports, which, being heavier than the suitcases, would receive a harsher treatment. They would receive more blows. I applied eight angles so that they would not burst on the first shipment.

The first box would accommodate the food. Only canned food went into the box. Space was reserved so that after the inspection of the Ministry of Agriculture at the Canadian customs, I could add rice, grains, and cereals and other items that I could not bring from Brazil. The Canadians controlled certain foods and prevented them from being brought in. The void area was filled in with bubble wrap to keep everything in the box in place.

The second box was also incomplete: it carried a machete, ropes, knives, pots, wire roll, screws, and tarpaulins.

In addition to food, I would need to purchase a chainsaw, fuel, stakes, ax, hinges, nails, a hammer, a crowbar, an inflatable canoe, two fishing rods, artificial bait and numerous other items that were on my list.

I could not forget anything.

I confirmed and reconfirmed everything multiple times.

The days went by. I was very impatient. My impatience lessened when the departure was near.

There is always, with a scheduled trip, an accumulation of services and responsibilities that we must ensure that in the absent period, we can leave companies and businesses in "relative" tranquility. This leaves us busy without having the wonderful sensation of making the final preparation and enjoying the anticipation that precedes such a trip that promises a dreamed for adventure that would last a little more than a month.

Arctic Adventure

At last, everything was ready, passport, visas and passages in hand, the day of departure arrived.

I arranged for Billy who helped me prepare for the trip and who was the driver in my company, to take me to the airport in the van.

He replied he could but laughingly asked if the van would hold everything?

"Yes," I replied. "Pick me up at home at 4:00 p.m. I want to arrive at Cumbica airport early. I will have excess baggage and I will need to register my rifle, cameras and equipment at the Federal Brazilian Customs."

That afternoon with all the baggage, we proceeded to the airport in São Paulo. On the way, the anxiety, and the realization that in less than twenty-four hours the change of weather would be immense.

A light drizzle was falling on our way from Santos to Guarulhos. Then on arriving in Sao Paulo we found a frightening congestion and a long delay. But Billy Joe knew the way well enough to find an alternate route.

It took two carts to hold all my luggage. The fine coolness of the Brazilian autumn was felt in São Paulo, it was a contrast with the warmer temperature of the coast of Santos. The pleasant weather seemed to welcome the trip to Toronto by Air Canada.

The time foreseen for document dispatch and the handling of excess baggage had not been calculated in vain. It is not every day that a passenger registers a hunting rifle to be carried inside a plane in Brazil. There were several Air Canada attendants trying to figure out the procedure to be used to properly register the gun. Luckily, it was before the "New York, September 11 factor".

Although the company is Canadian, the local employees were Brazilians and for them the procedure was extraordinary. The gridlock was solved when they called the manager, who already knew me and who had processed for the previous hunting trips that I had made. He only asked me to adopt the procedure of taking the rifle with the bolt removed and the rifle disassembled.

The ammunition was packed in a separate canvas with a padlock.

It seemed strange to embark on a hunting trip to Canada without my normal hunting traveling companions, my brother Conrado and my friend Lairton, with whom I had always shared most pleasant moments and memories from all the hunts we had done together.

This trip to Canada I would be on my own.

Finally, with bags and rifle checked and excesses baggage fees paid, I left Brazil with a Brazilian espresso coffee!

My adventure had begun. My anxiety drove me crazy. My seat barely fit my six-foot ninety-kilogram frame. Sleeping was impossible.

I sat awake and with several other insomniacs jealously watched an old gentleman open a real "sawmill".

The arrival in Toronto was nothing exceptional, except the pleasant sensation of arriving at a place that I like so much and where I was always so well received.

After declaring the reason for my trip, I proceeded to declare the entrance of a weapon and ammunition. The gun-case was not even opened and checked. I just filled out the document of the entrance of the weapon. I signed the clearance paperwork and made a payment for the rifle use fee. I was reminded that I would need the customs control paperwork to leave Canada. I was amazed at how easy the Canadians deal with a practice that does not exist in Brazil for political reasons where hunting has been banned for more than thirty years.

The fact that some countries allow a hunter to be able to hunt with correct regulations, is wonderful. All this tradition and sport should not be restricted for political or emotional reasons.

It is curious and amazing to know that ninety percent of the money for the construction and maintenance of schools as well as free Canadian education comes from the income generated from hunters and the license fees. Only ten percent of the revenue goes to the census, study, and balance of Canadian wildlife!

Arctic Adventure

After the customs inspection, I left all my luggage, the most that I have carried in all my life, outside of the customs area, in the baggage area. I did not need to worry about my luggage destination because in Sao Paulo I had checked in my bags to the final destination.

Although a wait in an airport is never very pleasant, I opted, for having a low stress connection with plenty of time between flights. After a few impatient waiting hours, I continued again.

The flight to Saskatoon, the largest city in the province of Saskatchewan was a four-hour flight. This city is larger than the provincial capital Regina.

On the flight, I had only some water and a biscuit. This is what I called a physically fit flight.

A few more hours separated me from the end of the day's journey. I had one more flight with Bearskin Airways to Camsell Portage, the northern most city in the province. Camsell Portage was equipped with an airstrip, about fifty kilometers from the border of the Northwest Territories.

This flight was worth memorizing. The aircraft built during World War II, with a capacity of 12 passengers, was a robust winged specimen worthy of a museum. The seats were like those of the urban buses of the nineteen sixties. The seats and backrest were covered by a shiny plastic so old that they had probably been covered in that time. They were a fixed tubular structure without any controls or ability to recline.

The luggage compartment was even more original. All the luggage was heaped between the cockpit curtain and the passengers. A nylon net fixed them between the floor of the aircraft and its side.

The engines were large contraptions compared to the size of the aircraft.

I was impressed by the communication service, when the pilot appeared with his face in the billowing curtain trying to make his voice stand out above the noise of the two "star" engines. He warned that we would take off soon and that we should all buckle our seatbelts and remain seated.

I was certain that the adventure had begun at that very moment when my world consisted of the deafening rumble of the engines, as they put all their energy trying to get enough speed to get off the ground. I was not wrong.

Despite the deafening noise of the engines, the plane seemed like it would not come off the ground. The sensation was more alarming when I began to feel the creaking and heard the internal noises caused by so many years of wear and tear and vibrations of the thunderous engines. It was a nightmare!

As soon as the plane left the ground. I felt the temperature drop sharply. At this time of year, on a flight at 5000 feet altitude, they did not turn on the heating.

The air entering through a crack in the floor, forced me to keep my foot on top of it to serve as a stopper. I could not move it. When I took my foot off the crack it felt like an icy fan was on. However, when I kept my foot on the crack, it seemed like I would freeze my foot. My foot went back and forth. It was a scene right out of a comedy movie.

It was a hopping flight, as we would call it in Brazil or the beating heart of a mother flight, the plane landed every twenty minutes or so. It would land for a few moments and then take off. Each time taking on or leaving some passengers or cargo.

Arctic Adventure

It was interesting that the cargo was often left unattended. It was placed at the runway windsock, which because often the runway was like a dirt track, was the only structure that indicated that there was an airport. It otherwise looked more like an unfinished dirt street.

These landings were not time consuming, they barely reached fifteen minutes. The first "stopover" was in Yorkton, where passengers descended in front of a shelter no larger than the size of a fifty-square-yard hovel.

Another stopover was in front of nothing, as it only had the runway, but some people were waiting by the side of the runway, where two vans complemented the scene, looking for load and the incoming passengers.

Several landings and departures later, the pilot looked more like a bus driver, because he took the tickets and controlled everything.

A few hours later, and I was now frozen, we landed at Camsell Portage airport. It was an airstrip where it had to be. The runway began on a beach on Lake Athabasca and ended at another beach on the isthmus.

Camsell Portage is a northern settlement of 37 people, located on the north-central shore of Lake Athabasca. The northern settlement is an unincorporated community in the Northern Saskatchewan Administration District.

This time the temperature in the plane was the same as the temperature into which I stepped.

As soon as I got out, I took some photos of the conglomeration of half a dozen houses and a canoe stuck in a warehouse into which only a very brave fisherman would walk.

Lost in these thoughts, I heard:

"You must be the Brazilian, no?", a bearded gentleman, with thick eyebrows and wearing a lumberjack hunting outfit, who appeared to be nearing the age of sixty, asked.

"Yes, but you're not Bill Petersen," I exclaimed!

"Yes. I'm certainly not Bill, young man," he said.

He pointed to where Bill was waiting for me by a van next to the runway.

That's right, right on the runway! Since the "airport" had nothing more than an unpaved lane, people with luggage wait by the side of the plane for some vehicle or someone to come and help remove it.

"Hi Manfred, how are you? Was it a good trip," Bill greeted me?

"Hi Bill, it's been a long trip and I'm feeling just like that square box door on plane. We are both beat up."

We both laughed at my bad joke.

Soon the pilot shouted from the door of the plane asking who belonged to the bags and boxes. Bill and his friend Josh retrieved the luggage and put them in the back of the van.

Arctic Adventure

The vehicle must never have been washed or seen water other than rain. It was filthy. The inside was a mix of spilled oil, dirty buckets, stumps of wood, and hoses. My luggage was shown no mercy and was put in by Josh and Bill. I looked at the van, then at Bill that was to be the seaplane pilot that would take me the next day to my destination. I wondered about the condition of his plane!

He would fly me to a small lake, among some thousands of lakes, and land at the foot of one of an unnamed and unknown mountain.

Thankfully, the saying "the first impression is the one that stays" turned out not to be true. I was scared by this first encounter.

I wondered how anyone who had a vehicle in such bad condition could have a reliable seaplane.

But upon arriving at his residence, where I would sleep on the first night, we met his wife. Mrs. Dorothy, a lady who greeted us and then apologized for not having arrived in time to return her husband's beautiful, 4 x 4, truck.

The one that picked me up belonged to the machine mechanic of "city". What a relief! I was also relieved when I found out this mechanic did not work on airplanes,

"Let's get inside," Bill invited.

As we entered the house, I came upon the residence of a legitimate Canadian from the "North": A Hunter, A fisherman.

I commented on the beautiful trophies and asked Bill if he had hunted them.

"Not all," Bill told me.

"The moose was my father's, he shot it when at the age of twelve he took me along hunting for the first time," he said.

From then on, the stories had no end. The many adventures around each trophy were proudly told in rich detail. I knew these were unforgettable moments for those who experienced them.

Accompanied by the crackling of the wood in the fireplace and a delicious red wine, we were served a delicious mushroom soup followed by moose meat cooked with potatoes in an irresistibly flavorful and seasoned sauce. So good that I twice repeated how good it tasted. I wondered when in the future I would enjoy such a good and exotic meal. And more frightening, I would have thirty days of Manfred as a "master chef"!

And, after dinner, a Blueberry pie for dessert! Blueberry, one of the bears' and my favorite foods.

After dinner. I went with Bill to check the items on the order list and to check on the arrangements previously requested and of course to reimburse him.

I asked Bill if the chainsaw was reliable.

"Yes, unless you decide to cut rocks " Bill said, raising only one eyebrow, as if to see what my reaction would be.

"Do I need to carry a spare blade or some spare parts," I asked?

"Absolutely," he said, raising both brows.

I was examining the chainsaw when Bill exclaimed with a laugh, "From what I see, you have a good trustworthy ax, it will be an excellent sleep maker after swinging it for a few hours in the pines. You will not hear the bears all night."

I replied that I was not sure how reliable this ax was and commented that I did not have any calluses in my hands anymore. Nor did I want to stop listening to the bears when they were close by."

Arctic Adventure

I checked the remaining items and tucked them into the crate. I left the chainsaw outside. Now, I thought, it's only six boxes and bags. When I got to the final destination, I could not forget anything on the plane.

"Here are the maps you asked for!" Bill said introducing me to three maps. Two of them were aeronautical charts. They were more complete and more detailed than the third one which was a road map.

As an airplane pilot, I could not help but to check the exact location and route to follow the next day. We were going up north. We would follow the 108th meridian West and go to just above the 60th parallel North. We would be next to the Arctic circle polar cap in the 65th parallel North.

Between exhaustion and anxiety, I finally went to lie down under a goose-down comforter at a pleasant temperature of sixty-six degrees Fahrenheit. Externally the thermometer registered forty-two degrees.

Ah, what a delight I thought. This is Canadian spring temperature!

Manfred Zepf

Diary Day 2:

Arrival at "Manfred" Lake

The sun with its rays still weak at this time of year, came through the thin curtains that veiled my sleep to wake me. I woke up new and refreshed! There is nothing like a good bed. My god, it was eight o'clock!

I walked quickly toward the living room and came upon Dona Dorothy and two other ladies sipping tea with toast.

"Hey, Sorry," I had forgotten where I was. I was still in my pajamas! I instantly turned around. I heard laughing behind me as I went back to the bedroom.

I went straight to the bathroom and then I saw that my hair was standing up like a porcupine!

Even though I was eager for the day ahead, I bathed. I wanted to take long enough to let those smiling ladies out.

That was my miscalculation. I was saluted in a "Good Morning" chorus, followed by smiles and "got caught".

Bill saved me when he said I'd have my breakfast on the plane. He said that we could not afford to waste any more time.

I checked on my luggage and wondered if I had forgotten anything?

Then Bill exclaimed, "That's all. Let's go."

"That's all. Let's go! I repeated as if answering my own question!

On the drive to the seaplane, we passed three irreverent bears. They were on the road and did not move off even as Bill honked as he approached. They were going to the place where the community threw out its litter and edible waste.

Bill explained that the bears were all over Saskatchewan. They were very dangerous and, they feared nothing and nobody.

"Every year there were some cases of someone being killed by a bear somewhere in the province.

"The school buses in Saskatchewan would now only deliver the children when an adult received them. And they were not allowed to carry any food in their lunch boxes.

"And beware of the swirling wind." Sometimes it blows to one side, where one should be more attentive, but always look 360 degrees," he continued!

We got to the hydrofoil. A Cessna 210 in apparent excellent condition - Phew!

Two gentlemen helped us load the luggage, gallons of fuel and my breakfast.

This time, my luggage was in first class. It was inside a "clean" bucket! And the runway was the smooth surface of the lake.

It was 9:30 a. m, everything was set, seat harness on, engine starting and the feeling of excitement. I was on the way to my adventure.

What a wonderful sensation. A dream of youth come to life at age of 35.

A mixture of anxiety and achievement for a unique, odd adventure that had a direction: North! The compass would point to the absolute North. A flight of around two and a half hours and then it would be time to choose a lake. We would probably baptize it with a name. It would be but one of the one hundred thousand lakes existing in the province of the Northwest Territories. This territory occupied one third of Canada's land area. This lake, I was sure would have the only inhabitant in hundreds of square miles around it.

"

Brigadier's Heaven", as we would say it in Brazil: There were no clouds at all. My breakfast consisted of scrambled egg with bacon that I ate with the toast.

"What the hell are you doing eating dry toast? Put the syrup on or it's a bad breakfast," Bill told me!

The syrup, though horribly sweet had a Vicks vapor rub mixed with honey flavor and that of some other unknown ingredients.

"I'm going to use syrup in the camp," I told him immediately after tasting it. It was a little lie because I hate syrup.

In Brazil we do not have the habit of eating much in the morning, but since I am the son of Europeans, I always ate a morning lunch.

"What a landscape, my god, what a landscape," I thought.

We were in an interspersed region of lakes and mountains, with no trace of humans for hours. Only at the takeoff, near Camsell Portage, did we see perhaps a dozen ranches.

It was already hard to say which was the most beautiful, which was the best, which was the ideal.

Because of their large size we noticed numerous elk along the way. They were easy to see from the air.

As the flight time reached the two-and-a-half-hour mark, I saw two lakes, a large one and a smaller one interconnected by a stream.

I pointed this out to Bill and suggested that the flat region between the lakes was an ideal location for the "camp."

"Let's take a flight around," Bill replied.

We took two laps to certify the conditions of the place and also of landing in the lake.

"Ok, that clearing is exactly what I want," I told him as I pointed it out.

High trees surrounded a clearing of ideal size for the construction of the bunker. It was on the "small" lake that had the area of one hundred soccer stadiums. The largest lake was a several kilometers long and surrounded the base of some beautiful mountains.

Flying low over the small lake Bill raised one eyebrow and asked if I wanted to land on "Manfred Lake?"

"The place looks perfect," Bill exclaimed.

"The lake is deep," he said. "We will not have difficulty landing, but are you ready to enter this "hot" water to land the luggage," he asked with a loud laugh?

"Okay," I replied as I pointed to a young moose feeding on grasses at the bottom at the far end of the small lake.

"Looking at dinner, huh?" That's a good idea," Bill said.

Bill examined the ideal place to land. He verified the direction of the wind as indicated by the small waves that formed in the lake.

What a lake I thought. Its water was an incredible translucent blue hue color made of the melting snow of the mountains that surround it. I believed that it was the purest water of the planet. The absence of human beings, the pure air, and the fact that the water descended the mountains in stone bedded streams that guaranteed their total purity.

A wonderful sensation and joy of being in this spot at this moment invaded my spirit.

Bill seemed to read my thoughts and commented,

"You chose well. The scenery is magnificent! And the climate here preserves, intact, a wonderful and indescribable place like this on the planet. You certainly will not find anything here to indicate that a human being has been here before. You will not even notice jets air streams crossing the skies. Here is the nothingness for civilization and everything for anyone who wants to be away from it. I love it," Bill exclaimed!

"It's this feeling that made me come to this country. I love this corner of the world. And I always say that I like my company. Sometimes it is very good to walk alone with your shadow," he said.

We skirted the wind leg, and Bill, humorously, picks up the microphone and asks for landing permission from the lake control tower. He calls them a nasty name because they ignore him and do not grant him landing permission. He laughs at his own joke.

The landing is smooth, and a rainbow of water sprays up from the landing floats.

Bill directed the seaplane into the clearing we selected from above. He peered through the open door, watched the distance from the floats to the bottom of the lake and the rocks.

"Bill, have you ever had the float stuck or chipped on a rock?" I asked.

He replied that yes in the past he had such a situation. He went on to say that it would be very bad to have problems with the float here.

He explained that the inside of the float was filled with polyurethane, but it still took in water and the seaplane was tilted. He had extreme difficulty in the takeoff. Since one float was more submerged than the other, the drag was difficult until the moment that the damaged float hydrodynamics left the condition of "a submarine" and began its skiing function. Bill said he had to compensate at the helm, and even then, he could not keep the initial trajectory of the takeoff against the wind. He had to make a quick turn to take off in a better direction.

He explained the damage to the ski happened when he scraped a submerged rock. Thankfully, he was taxiing because if he had been at speed, he would have ripped off the ski, and then maybe he would not be here today," Bill completed his story as he carefully moved toward the shore.

"And later at the time of landing, how was it," I inquired?

"I was very much afraid, for I did not know what reaction the aircraft would have when the float downed in the water. But thanks to the spigot in the hull of the ski, the water was draining from the moment it was in the air. This spared me an experience I would not want to have," Bill replied.

"Was it your only experience," I asked?

"Thank God, yes! And I would not want another at this end of the world," Bill exclaimed as he raised his two eyebrows.

"I'm already seeing rocks on the lakebed, close to the floats," I said.

"Yes, you're not the first to get that impression. We should be in about ten feet of water. These waters deceive. You will see when we are in water about twenty inches deep. That is when we have to turn off the engine and continue slowly to the beach." he replied.

So, it happened. Bill untied his seat belt and climbed onto the float.

He asked me to do the same before the floats scraped on the bottom of the lake.

He told me to jump in and to save the seaplane like a man.

I jumped into the water and held on to the seaplane.

I could barely avoid shouting, "What cold water !!!!"

Bill temporarily tied the plane to a large pine trunk located in the water. It had probably transitioned from the mountains to the lake in some past avalanche.

Soaked trousers and sneakers, we disembarked.

The boxes and baggage helped us eliminate the cold we felt on our legs and feet.

Bill helped me to transport them to where the camp would be erected. The location was protected from the wind at the edge of centuries-old pine trees in a higher part of the clearing.

Arctic Adventure

It was ideal for camping and raising a bunker, as it would be above the water level.

We ate a snack reinforced with roast moose and a juice prepared by Mrs. Dorothy. Apples were the dessert.

The adventure had begun and the next moment was one of urgent action. Our total effort was against time. It was about three o'clock in the afternoon and the temperature was beginning to drop.

We needed to build a shelter so that we could spend the night.

Initially I went to the edge of the lake, where with the chainsaw I cut a log in five pieces, each approximately four and a half meters.

With the machete I cut off the smaller limbs and used the ax to cut the thicker ones.

We pulled the smaller logs from the lake to the site for the structure by hand. Then we pulled the thicker heavier ones with a rope and pulley.

We had to do what Loshi, my Eskimo friend once did and what he taught me. We built a shelter that in Brazil could be said to resemble the shape of a bird's nest made of bamboo, but in the wilderness of Canada it had to be made with logs to protect us from the bears. The logs could not be too far apart. It was imperative that they could reach in between them.

The boxes and luggage were put in the middle and the structure was built around them. This was because the door would be just large enough for me to squeeze myself and my "small silhouette" buttock in from the top.

The arrangement is the same as a square where the first two logs are arranged parallel and staked into the ground. The two others would be parallel overlapping on the previous two and so on.

They were firmly lashed where they overlapped. We were overlapping and interlacing the logs until at dusk the beehive pyramid was completed.

Only the fuel and the tools for the construction of the bunker were outside of the 'new bunker".

Bill went to the lake and sank deep stakes to anchor the plane so it would be able to withstand the wind. Initially, in our first telephone conversations, he had indicated he would drop me off and return immediately to Portage. He decided to stay the night because he was concerned about returning at dusk when it would be hard to land. He had decided to stay overnight, when I asked him if he would help to make the bunker.

This would allow us to sleep safely on the first night.

It was fortunate that he stayed to help because with two people working hard, it was still a push to complete the bunker by end of the day.

This initial structure was where I would spend almost all the days of my adventure.

And for me, the adventure had to end well.

I was now prepared for my first night in that paradise.

Scented by the endless pine trees, a light breeze announced a cold night under a mantle of endless Northern Hemisphere stars.

I prepared a fire with the remaining logs, branches, and pine roots that we had gathered. I interspersed green and dry logs so that the fire would burn for most of the night.

I prepared my hot chocolate by hanging the pan over the fire in the Canadian way. It was a tripod of pine branches with the height and distance of the three legs so that they far enough away from the fire and not ignite.

A pan is attached with a wire that runs over the top and the ideal pan height can be adjusted.

In this style of cooking everything ends up with a somewhat smoky taste.

I made a fire inside of a circular stone wall about ten yards from where we would sleep. It was located toward the lake and was done so that the fire would not spread and threaten the forest.

The voracity of the burning logs was impressive. Feeling the intensity of the fire, I decided to put in some pieces of green logs so the fire could last longer. I put my cauldron to warm the water and I prepared to bathe.

Arctic Adventure

Bill incredulously said that I would die if I bathed at that hour. I said I had the habit of bathing, especially after a day of so much sweat.

How I asked was I to bathe at this temperature?

He recommended it be done with an improvised tarpaulin shower enclosure. This would be protection from the wind. Even so the bath needed to be very fast and the water at body temperature.

So that is what I did.

When I was done, I returned to the bunker and said,

"Bill, I agree the shower has to happen in the hottest hours, but this time I sweat too much, and I cannot sleep like that,"

He laughed and replied, "Yes, but I did not sweat like you since I do not have the courage to shower like you,"

The night had definitely arrived now. We were under a magnificent stellar mantle and experiencing absolute silence. Only the occasional crackling of the fire broke the silence.

I felt the sleep coming. I was tired. I stepped into a makeshift structure and tied the log on the top. This was the upper access entrance. I jumped into my "sleepy".". The last I remember was pulling the covers over myself. I slept wonderfully.

Bill settled on the cushions he'd taken from the seats of his plane along with some of the blankets he always carried. He went to sleep and opened a sawmill. Luckily after giving him a few shoves, he shifted, and I was able to sleep.

The protection from the log wall partly protected me from the chill wind of dawn. I had brought a tent, but I did not erect it, because it would not feel good to sleep inside it and leave Bill in the open. Nor did he want to sleep inside, we decided to protect ourselves with a tarp. There was no danger of rain, but the tarp gave me protection from the serene temperature of forty-one degrees Fahrenheit.

Manfred Zepf

Diary Day 3:

The Paradise from the Hand of God

At daybreak I woke up hungry.

I reactivated the fire. I told myself that there was almost no food to cook over the next campfire.

I prepared my first breakfast, with a coffee that Bill later told me kept him awake for at least another day. He was accustomed to what we Brazilians call "Chafe" because we see the cup bottom for Canadian and American coffee. Brazilian Coffee Bill classified as liquid asphalt paint that grows more than hair on your chest.

Do not worry about doing anything else because you have nowhere to replenish your stock! "He exclaimed, laughing!

"Manfredo, I'm leaving now," he told me.

"These are the coordinates of this location. I'll be back in thirty days. It may vary a few days if there are any bad weather conditions to get here. Rest assured, I will come to get you," he added.

Arctic Adventure

"Ok, Bill. Do not miss these coordinates otherwise I will have much work to get out of here. I think it would take about three to four months, and if I were luck, I would get to Camsell Portage alive if winter did not catch up with me earlier," I joked.

"No doubt," he replied, handing me a paper with the coordinates on them.

He then picked up the cushions, that came from is plane, and his blankets. He stepped barefoot, with his pants leg pulled up, into the cold lake water and walked out to the Cessna.

I was impressed Bill did not complain about getting into the water.

I walked in to help him. As soon as I entered the lake, I felt that the water was warmer than the temperature of the air, but the sensation of taking my feet out of the water was cruel.

"Bill, this water is cold, and my feet are turning purple," I exclaimed.

Bill laughed and told me to get used to it so I could take a bath.

"No bath in thirty days and I will not put you on my plane," he said with a laugh."

I helped him unhook the plane from the "anchors" as Bill called the stumps in the lake.

"Please do not remove the anchors." We'll use them when I get back," he instructed.

After untying the plane, we pushed the plane toward the center of the lake. He climbed on the float and then I saw that his feet were purple

"Your feet look like violet flowers," I said, laughing.

He looked at them as if he wanted to make sure they were really purple and then laughed with a shrug.

I stepped away from the plane as soon as Bill started the engine.

Bill went around the lake to get the engine to the ideal temperature. The floatplane cannot stand still like the others on the ground, because as soon as the engine starts up, even at idle speed, it keeps moving.

On his third round he smoothly took to the air.

I stood on the bank and followed him as if I were hypnotized. The spraying water mist at the moment of takeoff and the rise to the sky was beautiful.

Bill took off, made a turn, flipped over once as he went along the edge of the lake. As he went by, he flew by, waving the wings of the riders' fashion, alternating the level of the wings saying goodbye.

The moment I saw him disappear on the horizon a different sensation came to meet me. I realized that Bill was the only person who knew exactly where I was. Others knew of my existence and the direction we took, but no one knew exactly where Bill had left me. Nothing could happen to that pilot, especially on this venture. He would return to pick me up without reporting to any airport control tower.

After a few moments of reflection, I thought, "It's time to get to work!"

It was time to arrange everything. I began by leaving the rifle loaded and always at hand. I had to become aware at where I was. I had to have the bear at least five meters away to think of surviving an attack.

I set up my tent inside my shelter. There I would always be safe in relation to the bears and wolves, as well as the rains and inclement weather.

My next step was to reconnoiter the surroundings of the camp, to acquaint myself better on all the aspects of my environment. I needed more wood to improve my security and wood for the cooking fire.

Not far from the camp site, I was struck by the fury of a windstorm that, knocked down dozens of trees. It formed a corridor of downed trees in the middle of the woods. The storm had blown over a huge tree some thirty meters high. I would not have wanted to be around when that storm hit.

I returned to the camp and decided to inflate my inflatable canoe. I unpacked the pump and carefully stored the repair kit in the toolbox. The kit was very important and very valuable in this end of the world. It gave me relief to know that I had not forgotten it.

Arctic Adventure

I began to practice keeping an eye on what I was doing and another eye in the surroundings. It would be a healthy and prudent habit. I intended to practice and maintain this habit.

I inflated the canoe.

I tied it to the two "anchors" just as Bill had done with his plane. I did not want to scratch and damage my only means of water transportation.

I then prepared my fishing rod and put on an artificial bait. I tossed it to fish for my lunch. I hoped that like any lake in Canada, it must have fish too. At least that was my hope.

As soon as the bait fell to the surface, I was startled. That wonderful sensation of I caught one flashed in my mind.

The Line "sang in the water". The friction braked grudgingly released the line. Then a beautiful Northern Pike jumped nonstop to complete the spectacle. Five minutes of fighting and pulling him slowly in and then I pulled a nice lunch out of the water. I was impressed with the speed with which I caught the fish caught! It was measured in seconds.

After I caught the fish, I made my way back to the camp and a thought struck me. My god, I was reckless. I was about fifty meters from my shelter and my rifle.

What if I met a bear now?

And what if during my fishing when I was so excited a bear had appeared? It would have every chance to catch me unawares.

I would need to make it a habit to walk with my rifle as if it were a body suit. My rifle sling is padded, and I knew it would not bother me very much.

I prepared my first lunch. I only ate fish and more fish. I missed the memory of delicious fish cooked with lemon-lime spices. I had no lemon or limes. These items were not on my list of food to bring into the wilderness.

I threw the remains of the fish, the head, and internals and cast them into the lake. I did not want to create a land dump that would attract predators. This way the fish in the lake would have it as food.

In the afternoon I started the chainsaw and checked that it was ok.

Next thing, I thought, that I would check and get to know the surroundings of the lake.

But first I'll take my bath.

So, with the lukewarm water I went to my "Shower Box" to take my bath. It was a quick bath. You already understand the reason. The actual outside temperature did not help. And I did not want to go out and be surprised by bears.

The "Shower Box" I made, was about five-foot high, and about a three-foot square. I could barely fit.

I staked four stakes into the ground near a pine tree where the soil was spongy and where water would easily drain away. I stretched a plastic canvas that could be closed with only a hook.

Now again refreshed, I went to the canoe. This time I had my rifle hanging at my back.

It was time to paddle and learn the lake. It was serene and impressively beautiful.

One of the factors for choosing this lake was that the pine trees were near the water. I went down the lake to check out what I had seen from above. About three hundred meters from the camp, a wall of rocks, ranging from ten to thirty meters above the lake, sheltered hundreds of pine trees.

I completed the reconnaissance of the lake, where they had scenarios of stone beaches with the remains of trees, branches in the edge of the lake, ravines, cliffs, and escarpments.

What a beautiful place I thought. It was a wild beauty. I was sure no one had ever ventured around this place. I felt so because it seemed untouched, without human traces or pollution or environmental degradation.

It was the mirror of what God created. It was a rare spectacle.

I lost track of time as I observed and lived for the moment.

Then I hastened to return to the camp, for it would soon be night.

For dinner, I made an acorn rice that I ate with the rest of the fish.

I sat next to the fire and used the rest of green and dry logs.

Then it was time to brush my teeth and get into my sleeping bag and fall asleep.

It was a delightfully deep sleep.

Manfred Zepf

Diary Day 4:

Moose Meat and Two Bears

In the morning, the thermometer registered twenty-eight degrees Fahrenheit.

Blue sky and the crowded nightclub that surrounded me welcomed me on the second morning.

I was hungry and very thirsty. With my mug, I went to the lake. The water was delicious. Who says that water has no taste? The water was delicious!

I sat idly at the edge of the lake, waiting for the sun's rays to warm me through the haze that hung over the lake.

Good time for an encounter with elk I thought.

I did not even think twice. With my rifle on my back, I got into my rubber canoe and I left.

I made my way with little effort and without making a sound. I learned to paddle and to hunt in the native Brazilian villages. It is a paddling that requires patience. It is the art of plunging the paddle into the water without hitting anything and to also remove it without the water drops making any noise.

I went along the edge of the lake because the haze made it impossible to see farther than about 30 meters.

The water was filled with a weed that grew in the shallow water. The canoe made no noise as it passed through it.

I stopped paddling for a moment observing the beauty of this scenery. The canoe did not stop.

I heard water dripping, followed by a ripple. It was the sound that announced something moving through the water. My heart sank, and at the same moment I got my rifle from my back.

But I saw nothing, and the ripple came back after the noisy dive of "something big" in the water.

My heart became a loud drum beat in my chest and I could feel the pulse in my neck. My adrenaline skyrocketed into the stratosphere.

Then long minutes passed and there was nothing more. I cautiously paddled along the edge of the lake looking for what I was sure would be a moose. I again falling water, but this time it was nearer to me. I paddled in the direction of the moose.

I had seen a moose from the plane, and this very place where I now thought I might have heard a moose was it. I looked straight ahead through the fog.

Then a large moose appeared some twenty meters away. It was standing still as it recovered its breath. It had a mouthful of aquatic grass and bulbs. It seemed to be letting the water drain back into the lake. It was making the noise that is so characteristic of this animal.

He plunged down into the water again.

I took advantage of this moment to move to a better location. I avoided any sudden movement or noise that would alert the moose. I stepped out of the canoe into the water. I focused the telescope and fired the rifle. The moose plunged inert and died painlessly, for my shot was accurate and struck him in the head.

I thought, my stock of meat was guaranteed.

Yes, the biggest problem now was that this young moose probably weighted around one thousand pounds. It was much different from an adult moose that could reach a twice that size but the question and the problem for me was how to get a half ton moose from the lake by myself?

I immediately went to the bank and marked the location with a branch, so I could find it when I returned. I went back to the camp to get ropes, my machete, and a sharp knife.

I wondered how I would get the animal out of the lake.

The moose would not float. So, I would have to have a way to pull him from the water. Dragging the moose in the water seemed almost impossible. I was also worried about the distance through the woods that I would have to travel if I did get it to shore and took it back to camp. It would not only be very tiring but also it would be very dangerous for two reasons.

First, moose was a favorite food for bears and wolves, and they would pick up the scent from a great distance.

Second if they found me moving moose carcass, I would surely have to shoot to kill these predators for the carnivorous appeal would be immense.

There would be another factor that would also accentuate the danger. My hands would be shaking from the effort of pulling the moose and taking an accurate shot would be almost impossible.

No, it really was not wise to move the Moose by land.

There was only one option, I would clean the moose by the lake and section it into manageable pieces that could be taken little by little by canoe back to the camp.

I could not believe that I would have to dive about two meters down in ice cold water to tie a rope to the one of the Elk's legs. Then I would have to pull it out of the lake on my own.

Arctic Adventure

When I returned, I ran back and forth along the edge of the lake without stopping. When I thought I was warm enough, I took off my coat. I was trying to prevent going into thermal shock. Every piece of clothing I took off was already a drama, but when I set my feet into the water my teeth started to chatter.

I had the rope in my hand, and I went in. The shock and suffering from the cold air and the freezing water was overwhelming. I thought I was going to die. That is when I thought "if not now when?" I was almost totally in the water. The answer to my question was "if not now when?" would be never.

I went farther in and then felt the moose with my feet. I immediately dived down into the water. I immediately resurfaced in need of oxygen. I plunged again into the water and was able to put the loop on one leg. I secured the second hind leg on the next dive.

I exited immediately and scraped off the water from my body and began putting on my clothes. By this time, my feet that seemed to have suffered the most and had given me the most pain began showing signs of life.

Finally, it was time to pull the moose out of the water. I did not think it would be too difficult. The stone bottom of the lake had smooth plants that would surely help the moose's body slip over them. I set my feet on a rock and pulled. I was not able to budge the moose even an inch.

I decided to go back to the camp to get two pulleys. I had to use brains over brawn. I returned from camp and arranged a pulley system that would help me get the moose out of the water.

Because I did not want to get back into the water, I used the canoe to tie a pulley as close to the moose as I could. I connected the other end to a nearby pine tree. The setup was perfect, but I was alone, and the moose was very heavy. Even using the pulleys, the operation proved to be very difficult.

It was a long half hour struggle. I used the lever method, and a truck driver's or climber's slip knot system, to slowly pull the heavy moose from the water.

Then with my faithful hunting knife, I cut the moose into pieces I could handle and carry on the inflatable canoe. Nothing was wasted. Everything was properly handled.

The parts that we humans dislike is to other animals a delicacy. I did not bury the remains but left the discarded parts in two different places. This was my attempt to avoid disputes between wolves and bears. The law of survival of the jungle had continuity.

The sun was still high, and I estimated that it was close to noon when I finished the last trip with the moose. I proceeded to set up a place to hang the meat. I used the knowledge shared by my Eskimo friend and chose two pines about six feet apart and about fifteen feet up I tied a heavy rope between them. I hooked a pulley in the middle. Then I hoisted each piece of the moose and anchored them along the rope. When I was done, I covered the meat with a tarp so that the crows did not attack the meat.

Finally, I was done! Even with the pine trees quite arched by the excess weight, the moose was about five meters from the ground. I thought this was high enough that a bear would not be able to reach it from underneath.

Moose meat looks like beef. It has the same consistency, but I think it has a better taste. It has the advantage of not having toxins nor the fat of farm raised beef.

I revived the campfire with the wood that I had gathered for my "kitchen". I set my makeshift tripod over the fire and went to fetch water from the lake. I was surprised because the water seemed to have a pleasant temperature.

I put the water to boil.

By this time, I had taken off my coat. I was sweaty from the hard work of getting the moose back to the camp and hoisted into the air. I decided to bathe in the lake. I planned to stay close to shore where the water would be a little warmer than out in the lake.

It was my first bath in the lake.

Wow, what a relief. After a rejuvenating bath, I returned to cook my dinner.

I prepared a seasoning and put it in the boiling water. Then I made delicious "soaked" rice that I liked. On my grill, I prepared a delicious and juicy moose steak.

Wow, how I ate.

I felt the shadow of a centuries-old pine tree and almost fell asleep. But the squeaky sound of the crows wanting to catch the moose's flesh gave me an alarm. I had to worry about the bears.

Yes, I could not neglect staying alert. The odor of the moose meat was now a strong lure. The odor would spread even farther from its lofty height. And the racket being made by the crows would alert the bears as well.

I went to the bunker and took a delightful nap. The evening cold provided a natural alarm, but the sun was still in the sky and there was still time to do some work.

I was surprised at how long I had slept.

Quickly, I began to separate the tools and materials that I would use the next morning to start the construction of the cabin.

I cut some of the low limbs of the pine trees that surrounded the area where I planned to erect a cabin. Then I used a hoe to clean and prepare the ground until the sun went down.

In the firelight, I updated my notes as I enjoyed the evening and drank a hot mug of chocolate. Certain that it would not rain, I took down the tent and lay down looking up at a wonderful stellar mantle. A small breeze gently touched the branches of the pine trees. What a perfume, what a night. I then pulled the canvas to protect myself from the dew. I did not even realize when I fell asleep.

Suddenly I woke up. What's going on???

I heard something scraping on the bark of the logs of my bunker. Yes, no more than two meters separated me from the threat, and something was there. Who was trying to enter?

I heard it rising from right to left, past the entrance smelling and gasping at the same time.

Frightening! Yes, I thought. In fact, I did not even have time to think much. It's a bear, surely a bear was trying to get to me.

By the faint light of the bonfire, the immense silhouette of another bear was trying to find food. This included me as I huddled inside my cage.

Wow, I thought a bear invasion? Yes, there were at least two.

I could not hesitate. I had to make some decision about what to do. Yes, I needed to act quickly and efficiently.

Already reasoning better, I took my rifle and decided to strike the bear in the belly in the attempt to frighten it and make it leave. The bear gave the rifle a swift and sure kick that launched it to the other end of the bunker.

This was my worst moment. I did not know what happened to my rifle. In this part of the world, it would be impossible to stay and survive without a it. I figured that if the scope had been broken, I would still have the traditional sight. But if some other vital parts of the rifle were damaged, I would be in a bad situation.

At that moment there was nothing I could do.

Yeah, I thought, where did I leave my flashlight? Yes, it was in my backpack by my side. With my flashlight, I began to identify the situation. The bear was huge, with claws that were even more frightening. It kept trying to grab the log gap or something edible with its sharp nails.

Immediately two things crossed my mind. Would the ropes hold the kicks and bites that this beast was throwing? And would the logs hold? Surely, the bear had been attracted by the moose, and since it cannot reach it, the smell of blood had stirred them, and they were excited.

When the bear made a focused and insistent attempt to get some food from my food box (potatoes, onions, fruit, among others) at the opposite end of my bunker, I jumped quickly toward my rifle.

Was the rifle whole? What about the telescopic sight? I returned promptly to the center of the bunker. I examined the rifle with one eye and kept the other eye on the brute. Apparently, nothing had happened to the rifle. I cocked it!

I looked out at the campsite. Not even the burning fire within a few yards of the bunker where I was sleeping intimidated these savages.

I felt the panting and the despair of the bear followed by a hoarse guttural roar. It was as if the bear was despairing at having the food so near and "appetizing" and the impossibility of getting its claws on it.

"I'll shoot up in the air, and if I do not intimidate him, I'll have to kill him," I thought.

Then I heard the crack of a tree breaking and a thud. Was it the fall of the pine or the sound of the moose, crashing into the ground?

My insistent bear stopped immediately and ran toward the sound.

This gave me a break and I got my thoughts in order.

What was happening?

I wondered if one of the was able to reach the moose and break the tree?

Had he gone by a rope?

Impossible, I could not believe it.

Perhaps there were more bears.

"A couple of bears was about right," I thought. "Bears do not flock.

I tried to see through the cracks in the logs to the pines on which I had hung the moose. The bears were hidden by shrubs. From time to time, they appeared to glitter between the bushes. Their eyes glittered as they turned toward my flashlight. I had confirmation when two pairs of eyes reflected as they looked at me.

I could not sleep. I knew I was no longer in danger, for the two "Ursus horribilis," the scientific name for the grizzly bear, were satisfied to focus on their feast. As soon as I was able to see that they had left the camp, I untied the log that closed my protected space.

I got out of my bunker and decided to check out my rifle. There didn't seem to be any external damage to the rifle or any damage to the scope. There were no marks on the rifle. I think I was very lucky because the rifle either struck with the butt or the end of the barrel on some log.

I propped up my rifle and fired a shot to check it out. The shot was accurate. The rifle had survived undamaged.

Thank you, Oh God!

With my woodpecker, the nickname I affectionately gave to my rifle, I walked around the campsite to survey the damage.

Impressively, two bears practically ate all the elk's quarters and even invested a few bites in the ribs.

It seems that the weight of the moose that I had hung on the clothesline rope bent the two pines quite a bit.

One of the bears using its huge claws climbed into one of the pines. Its weight and the weight of the moose flesh caused the tree to break.

It must have given the bear a great shock. Its great agility must have saved it from a fracture.

Bears climb trees with the ease of cats. They can run at up to thirty-five miles per hour and they have the smelling ability forty times more powerful than a dog. This is the profile of this omnivorous mammal that reigns supreme in the forests of the northern hemisphere. It is the "absolute master" of this region.

It has no natural predator.

It is feared and respected by all the natives of the northern provinces of Canada.

Loshi used to say, "when you take a gun and go hunting the big bear, you are actually being hunted by it," or "he does not even fear the fire," and he concluded by saying that "the only time he is harmless is during the salmon spawning season when he is ten yards away and he is in pursuit of his favorite dish. But do not get any closer than ten yards! The bear will think you might want to take his precious food from him and attack."

Wise words that sum up experiences of an unfriendly relationship of the Eskimo people with these giants that can reach up to seventeen hundred pounds.

Loshi told me a lot of stories and what I forgot probably saved the bears last night.

It is interesting, that the moment I thought about shooting up in the air to scare the bear with the huge boom caused by the 30-06, that at that exact moment the pine seems to have identified with the "spirit of the forest" and protected them by breaking.

The Eskimos say that bears may be the spirits of their ancestors wandering in the forest. Loshi's relatives said that, "They do not appear, they arise! And just as they arise, they may disappear."

Coincidence or not, the bears seem to have followed this path and in this past night's adventure I lived through a unique experience that had moments of maximum adrenaline.

The outcome left my meat supply at zero. This meant that another moose was needed. I'd have to hunt for another. But this time I would not shoot one in the water.

After an inspection of the camp, as a survivor of this stormy night attack; I ate a deserved apple, accompanied by crackers and a legitimate Brazilian coffee to bolster my survivability.

Manfred Zepf

Diary Day 5:

Cabin Logs and Northern Lights

Get to work, I thought.

I scanned the place where the future bunker would be erected, and with the measurements in my head, I went out looking for the ideal tree trunks. I would cut them in the northern part of the lake, where I could drop them from the top of a rock formation that I called the "tip of the Headdress."

It really looked like a headdress. The silhouette in the morning made the crooked and hanging pines on the rock have the feather shapes of an Indian headdress. This rock formation, a precipice of free fall for the trunks, was perfect. They would fall from the height of about sixty-five feet. I was certain the water was deep. Even though the water was translucent, I could not see the bottom. I was certain that I could drop them without fear that they would touch the stony bottom of the lake.

I chose to cut down trees back away from the cliff. I wanted to drop the trees where I could cut off the branches. Otherwise, it would be impossible to transport what I had cut back to the camp. Cutting the branches in the water would be an impossible task and very wet.

I cut the smaller branches with the machete. The thicker ones were more difficult, and it was necessary to use the axe or the chainsaw. I cut and cleaned the first tree. I spent half an hour to make three perfect logs from this first tree. I cut and fell the tree so that the top was uphill and the bottom closer to the lake.

Despite the weight of the first log, I was able to launch it into a forty-five degree fall to the lake. As the sun rose toward its zenith, I was able to cut, clean and throw fifteen green pine logs into the lake. It felt very good to see that I managed to do this on my own.

I also threw in a twenty-foot-long dry pine log. I planned to make a stool and a lunch and dinner table with it.

It was now time to float the logs back to the camp. I was using the inflatable canoe to tow the logs.

I tied the logs linearly. The end of a log to the beginning of another and so on. Since I did not want to cut the rope, I was only able to tow eight logs.

I tied the rope around my waist. I did not want to chance tying it to the canoe and take a chance on damaging it. I started rowing. In the first ten strokes I advanced a little more than a meter. But with consistent paddling, I managed to reach a reasonable speed. Then I paddled only hard enough to maintain a constant speed.

As I approached the camp, I untied the rope from my body and tossed it to the right side and guided the canoe away from the logs. The logs floated safely by toward the rocky beach.

I untied them from each other and placed each log at least one meter up on the rocky beach.

I coiled up the rope and put it into the canoe.

I went to the camp and this time it was not the giant bear that was attacking but a much smaller adversary. Squirrels! Yes, little squirrels were stealing my cookies and breads. How could they? The big and strong bear tried and could not rob me of the food inside my shelter. The irony was that these animals of few grams of weight boldly took my food from the box. I ran behind them shouting like a mad man, threw rocks and sticks to frighten them away. I wanted them to be afraid to venture into my camp and steal my biscuits and breads.

"At least their presence was a guarantee that there was no bear nearby," I thought.

"Now," I thought, "I'm going to see if there's still some fish in this lake and I'm going to prepare my lunch."

I took my fishing rod and went to the lake to cast my line and to get some lunch. With the reel unlocked, the bait flew out a long distance. As soon as I reeled the line tight, it was clear that a fish had already been hooked. I reeled it in, and a three-kilogram northern pike jumped, dived, and fought for of a few minutes out over the lake.

I thought that I had managed to catch my lunch. Wow, I thought, I will not be able to eat it all for lunch and I do not want to eat fish again for dinner. I returned him back to the lake.

I threw out my line again. Again, while taking up the slack another northern pike was on my hook. Only on the fourth cast did I catch the fish that matched the size of my appetite.

The experience was overwhelming. I had never had the experience of fishing in such a spot that was so rich in fish. It seemed that I was fishing in an "aquarium." But fishing in an aquarium would have been monotonous. Here though it seemed that every cast was successful, and every fish put up a good fight.

I finished my lunch and no food remained for any large or small, unexpected visitors. But the hundreds of fish bones made me wish for the bigger fish. The next time I would choose the bigger fish.

I picked up my rope put it in the canoe and then pushed my canoe into the water. I paddled north again back to where the rest of the logs were located.

Arctic Adventure

I paddled without making noise as was the custom of paddling by the Indians in the river hunts in my country. It was a practice that always brought good results to hunters. Good results were what I would need for this adventure.

A black bear mom with her cub were eating from the bones of the elk that I had left.

The only movement that occurred when they noticed my presence was a guttural sound that the mother bear made to her cub. It promptly climbed the first pine tree it found. It stopped when it got to the top. The cub then looked down at its mother with a suspicious look. She was not intimidated by my presence or by the canoe and continued to eat. She just would not turn her back to me.

I got a little closer to the bank but remained at a safe distance. If she came toward me, she would have to swim much of the way, which would give me time to paddle and get away from her claws. I knew she would not do it because she would not leave the cub. She was its protection from it turning into food for a passing male bear.

As I got closer, she paused to look at a being that I was sure she had never seen. She lifted her nose and seemingly attempted to identify my scent. I was up wind from her and did not have to smell her. She then walked slowly toward the tree in which held the cub. She then turned to me to make sure what was happening.

I paddled on and left them and went back to get the logs I had come for. A few moments later I looked back and noticed that the mother bear and the cub were gone. She probably left for safety reasons.

It is important to point out that the mother bears are brave. From the moment they are born, until they reach a size where they can defend themselves, the bear cubs are for the father or any other male bear nothing more than food. That's it. If the mothers are not exceptionally brave the males would eat the cubs.

This may seem inconceivable to us. We grew up in the city reading comic strips where we saw tender and thoughtful bears. Bears became the idols of an entire urban generation who were clueless about the true nature of a bear's life.

As a child we have all been told stories that always end with "and so they lived happily ever after". And no one to deny them in the future! Then we finally find out when we grow up that real life is very different from the story.

We learn that the law of survival and it seems cruel to our eyes and instincts, but the balance of nature also teaches us, that they kill to eat. I am sure that if they could speak, they would surely express surprise that there are beings that think but kill for anger, for love, for power.

When I got to the logs, I tied them together as before. Then I again tied the rope to my waist and began to row. This second trip seemed as if I was pulling twice as many logs as I had done in the morning. It was clear that I was getting tired.

I used a pulley to pull the logs out of the water so they could begin to dry out. This would make them lighter and easier to handle. Cut logs lose up to forty percent of their weight in a few weeks due to the loss of water.

By the time I got done I was in a sweaty condition and knew that I needed a bath. In my hot and exhausted condition, the water at the edge of the lake was almost bearable.

The night was coming, and sleep was coming again. High-altitude clouds, cirrus stratus formed in the sky. "It will probably rain for the next few days," I thought. At least if I saw such clouds in Brazil it would be.

I ate two bananas, but they had no taste, "nothing of nothing", was the saying in the big beautiful and lovely city of Santos where I live.

I ate plain rice. I did not want to open the canned goods yet. And I closed dinner with a box of orange juice.

I lit the fire, and I enjoyed its warmth.

When sleep was about to overtake me, I went to the lake to get water to brush my teeth. When I bent down to dunk the pan and collect water, I experienced the unique scene of the northern lights reflecting off the mirror like surface of the lake.

A shiver that went through my whole body. No matter how much I try to describe the beauty and wonder, I would still fall short of the reality and emotion that I felt with this ballet, with this dance of lights. The colors ranged from blue to yellow tones, from yellow to green, to lilac, to pink, and then to white. They say the lights are due to a magnetic pole effect. When they arise, because they arise, everything is mystical and mysterious in relation to their presence. They are seen only in the northern hemisphere, close to the polar cap.

Arctic Adventure

I stood for what seemed like forever in astonishment and amazement. Only the cold brought me back to the reality and realization that I needed to wrap myself up.

I lay down by the dying fire. Only embers burned lazily. I did not want the brightness of the fire to diminish the eternal beauty of that moment. In the euphoria of seeing this spectacle of lights, I did not immediately put the last log from above, which would be "my door" to better observe the "northern lights" the beauty up above. Then without realizing it, I slept!

I slept wonderfully, and I was lucky for the grizzlies who visited me two nights before did not return.

Leaving my door open scared me. Mistakes like that can be fatal.

I could not neglect safety.

Manfred Zepf

Diary Day 6:

Destructive Visitors

In the morning, after eating two oranges, I fried an egg that I ate with a slice of bread.

I was feeling very good.

A few low clouds floated across the sky. "I think we're going to have a spring rain," I thought. The pure air and total absence of people, noise, and any personal commitments really felt marvelous. I have always lived well by myself and today, with a veil of clouds under the sun, not even my shadow was with me.

I did not feel as cold as I did the first day, and I no longer had any "thermal shock" when washing my face in the cold lake water.

I took the dry log, cut my bench from it, and decided to make boards and beams from the rest so I could build a table. Yes, how odd you may think, that I made a table before I started the house. I needed a comfortable place to eat to keep up my strength to build the cabin.

I needed more firewood. I had the remains of the wood used to make the table, but I would have to gather more wood.

Because I wanted to use the chainsaw only for what was necessary and because I was afraid to run out of gas before finishing the construction of the cabin, I went out with only the machete, the axe and my faithful 30-06.

I went to that corridor of felled pines that seemed to form a road or perhaps an avenue.

After a dozen good looks around at the surroundings to make sure I was alone, I began with the ax making several blows and I cut the tip off a pine tree that was close to the edge.

This was the ax and the machete that I had given to my brother-in-law in Brazil to sharpen. Carmelo sharpened them so well that when he gave them back, he joked that I would not need to take a razor to shave. Despite the exaggeration about the sharpness, I was really impressed and enjoyed using them.

Between each movement and action, I carefully watched the surroundings. I did not neglect this. It was now already a habit, but when I saw some bear droppings around, I was even more alert.

The smaller branches and limbs I cut with the machete. I was collecting the smaller branches to use to start the fire. There is nothing better than small dry pine twigs to start a fire. They contain a highly oxidizing resin, and they are highly flammable.

When a fire starts in the forests of these regions there is no way to put it out. All it takes is a lightning bolt in a storm to hit some dry pine, and the fire rages. This is one of the greatest dreads of the Inuit.

In a short amount of time, I had cut a week's worth of small limbs. I tied them up into a big bundle. After that I began to cut the top end of the pine tree.

The echoes the sound of ax blows rang through the forest. They made a sound different from the woodpeckers. I thought that even the curious animals preferred to flee from the sound of the blows of the axe.

I arranged the wood into two piles and attached two beams that would allow me to carry the load balanced on my shoulders. About a third of the load was made up of smaller limbs. It was exactly what I could carry.

Before picking up the load, I scanned the surroundings.

Yes, a bear! He was standing a little more than one hundred feet away on his back legs with his two front paws out in front of his chest as he watched me.

The noise must have attracted the bear. It appeared, suddenly from nowhere.

Without blinking my eyes, so as not to lose sight of the bear, I put the bundles of wood down. I tried to make as little noise as possible, but I did not think it mattered because the bear had already seen me.

Now I had to be precise, cunning, and quick.

With my hands free, I quickly pulled my rifle from my back.

And what I feared happened. The bear disappeared! It was among the fallen trees, which provided perfect cover, and it knew it.

As a result, I did not know where the bear might come from. And as I have mentioned before, they are fast and can reach up to thirty-five miles per hour!

I immediately had the rifle safety off, and my rifle cocked. I began to try to think like a bear.

What would I do to get to my feast?

Within seconds, I decided to walk slowly until I was about thirty feet away from the fallen pine trees. I leaned against a large pine tree that would cover me in case I was attacked from behind.

I was looking across the area of all the fallen trees. I knew that the bear would not expose itself if it decided to attack. It would most likely come from the area that provided some camouflage. I consistently scanned the area in front of me from left to right. I anticipated an attack from the right. The trees had been blown over to the right and the tree roots on the left side provided little camouflage.

I quickly scanned back and forth in what seemed to be an eternity. An eternity that more likely was no more than a few minutes.

I thought that he could not have given up on me.

Then as I glance back to the left, I was amazed, shocked and my adrenaline shot to the clouds.

I wondered how the bear got out of the area of fallen trees and had come unseen toward me?

No, it seemed impossible. The bear was about forty yards away walking directly toward me. I was impressed with its ability to move without a crack of a twig, without a single noise. It was truly impressive. I saw the calmness with which it walked. I still didn't hear a sound. It was rather frightening to see the bear walking towards me.

I thought about throwing a stick to distract it and make it look in the direction of the throw. But the bear already had me in its sight. And I could not spare a hand to throw the stick.

I had to concentrate.

The thought that there could be more than one bear made me look quickly around. The time which may have been minutes seemed like an eternity of hours.

The bear paused, raised his snout so that he could sniff and make sure of his prey. It took a few more steps, and my rifle scope cross hairs were already pointed in the center of his head. I made no sudden movements or noise so that I would not be located precisely.

The bear stopped and again began to sniff.

I knew this bear was dangerous it had not been alarmed by the sound of the axe. Most probably it had been attracted by my scent from miles and miles away. My scent must have been associated with that of a fine banquet. A banquet that would satisfy the Bear's immense and voracious appetite. I knew that the bear would not likely change its mind. I could not hesitate for a single second.

What was I going to do? If I gave it a warning shot and then the bear could attack me, and I would not have time to reload. The extremely agile bear would be able to get to me before I would be ready to fire again. There is no other way. If this "Ursus horribilis" took one more step in my direction I would have to kill it to save my skin.

The bear with its myopic vision was confused about my exact location. It was still as a statue listening and sniffing once more for me.

What would the bear do?

In a fraction of a second, it could take a variety of attack actions. It had hardly come here to give up easily on me.

What could I do to try to frighten this lord omnipotent in its habitat? Nothing I thought, there was nothing else I can do. I would have to kill it. I lowered my head to put the sight's cross hairs on the bear's skull. I was focused and within a fraction of second of pulling the trigger when the bear looked to my right and jumped suddenly to its left and ran quickly from the woods.

What had frightened the bear? I thought whatever it was must be nearby.

If this big bear ran, imagine what scared him? It was now beginning to be extremely dangerous. It was now dusk making my vision difficult. If I did not get out of the area quickly, I knew I might not leave alive.

I saw the movement of the new bear at a distance. I knew it must be bigger than the first one, since it frightened that bear away immediately. This bear was probably the "owner of the place."

Without even blinking, I looked at the edge of the pine tree next to his head and squeezed the trigger. I wanted the shot to rip part of the bark off and be the target of the bear's retaliation.

The very loud noise of the shot left me momentarily deaf, and I could therefore not hear whether it had run or not. Through the telescopic sight I could see that it was gone but I could not determine the direction the bear had taken.

The gunpowder smoke drifting in air was an indicator of the bear's direction. In less than two seconds I reloaded my rifle and was again ready. This was critical in case the bear attacked. Being ready swiftly was critical. That is why I have trained on having speed to accompany the precision of action and aim. This is the ability that guaranteed my life.

But I did not find anything to do with my cocked rifle. I did not in cold blood want to kill a bear unnecessarily. With the help from up above this time I was able to avoid killing without necessity.

I looked in every direction. It seemed that there were three lucky beings. Each left the area alive. Perhaps frightened and hungry but alive.

I took up my bundles of wood but on the way back stopped to look at where the bullet had hit the tree next to the bears head.

It was clear to me that the bullet had ripped the bark and four deep claw marks swept across that spot the bullet hit. The bear probably thought the attack came from that spot. Even though it had been risky, it validated my strategy.

It had been about a fifty-yard shot and I had my rifle ready for action again in seconds. I had been able to prepare in case it had decided to attack me.

I returned to the camp and piled and covered the wood.

Then with my faithful "woodpecker" hanging on my back I paddled the canoe back to the "headdress" in search of more logs that I would cut and would throw into the lake.

The lake no longer had the usual blue hue. It was greener, greyish.

I cut the same number of logs as the day before, but I decided not to take them to the camp until later.

I quickly returned to the camp because I was as hungry as a lion.

I took my pole and cast the lure to choose the right-sized fish for lunch. I decided with a chuckle that this time I would take the big fish. I readily agreed with the size of the first fish even though it was much larger than my appetite.

Once fried, I was happy to have had more success with the big bones. The bones were easier to deal with.

I sat for a while on the edge of the lake, which now had small undulations formed by a gentle wind. I thought that the northern wind would probably bring in the cold air and that it might rain for a few days.

I decided it would be a good idea while it was dry to devote myself to cutting more logs. I would be able to stand under a canvas and cut notches into the logs when it rained.

I ate quickly and went back to the "Headdress" and quickly cut twenty-eight logs. I again tied the logs up so that I could tow them back to camp. On my third trip I noticed that I had only had five logs for my next tow.

"I don't understand," I said to myself.

I counted twenty-eight logs and now there are only twenty-six. I could not see any logs down in the water. I was sure that I had watched the fall of all of them.

I was curious and keen to understand this mystery.

I decided to return with the five logs. As I paddled by the place where I left the remains of the moose, I saw six wolves fighting over the food. I knew they were everywhere, but until this moment I had not seen them. They are ill tempered, as the "Inuit" say, and that's why you cannot give a damn.

After beaching the logs at the beach by the camp, I went with the mountain chainsaw and the rifle to the site of the dry pines toppled by the storm. I baptized the place as "Bear Avenue".

It looked just like an avenue because the clearing in the woods was linearly perfect on both sides and two bears greeted me here the last time.

I was more attentive and aware of the place this time. I verified that a lot of the bear droppings on the ground among the logs were very fresh. This gave me a bit of concern. I had my chainsaw in hand instead of my rifle.

With the chainsaw I cut the pieces that I wanted to use to make the roof beams. The thicker branches would supply the cooking fire. The green pieces would help in keeping the fire burning longer while the smaller dry ones helped in getting it started.

I took the two harnesses bound by rope. I wondered if the noise of the chainsaw scared the bears. No, I was sure it did not.

It was already getting dark when, upon returning to the camp, I saw my coat near the edge of the lake. Immediately I looked toward the camp. Yes! There were two bears!

One was a very large one, perhaps ten years old or more. His belly was so big it looked like it was going to scrape on the ground. I think the younger one, was a female, because she was always behind. She was not as big but certainly she was around seven or eight years old.

I had been warned not to be careless. I had left camp and left my bunker open.

I had a hunch these two were the same ones that had feasted on my elk. They were really destructive.

Upon realizing this, I immediately put my load down. They did not hear to me, maybe because of all the noise they were making in my makeshift kitchen. They ripped the protective plastic from the sides of the bunker and knocked down pots and everything they saw.

What was I to do? They had not yet perceived my presence. It gave me time to think. I was in their habitat and even with the gun cocked I was out matched. There were two of them.

"I will have to rely on my intelligence," I thought, "They no longer have a moose to entertain them, and today I will be their favorite menu."

I did not know if I would be able to avoid having to shoot them, but I had to try. It was getting dark, and I did not have the flashlight with me. I had my waterproof matches, candles and compass, items that I always kept in my hunting jacket. There was nothing I could do with these items.

I was safe if they did not notice me. And they would most likely notice me very soon.

I was hiding behind a very old pine tree with branches starting about three feet from the ground. I did not hesitate. I took off my boots and with the rifle on my back I climbed up noiselessly, branch after branch, without taking my eyes off the two. I had left my boots on the ground because I could climb quietly in my socks and in case of an attack the boots would serve as the first decoy.

I stopped climbing when I was about twenty feet off the ground. Even though they had not yet seen me, as I now getting into their sight. The biggest of the two stopped in the midst of the mess they had made. He began to sniff the air. This was a warning to me because it was clear he had identified something strange. Either he heard me or because I was up higher, my scent reached his nostrils.

"Maybe it was the strong smell of gasoline from the chainsaw," I thought.

I stood with the gun resting on a branch always pointing in the direction of his head.

I concentrated on the male. The female continued to search for food. The male knew that he was smelling something unlike anything he had ever known. The smell of an unknown being, the curious smell of petrol, orange, bananas and apples, fried foods, all at one time.

The bear looked from side to side and snorted non-stop.

I wondered what I should do. Surely, he would soon come after me. He would not come at a gallop, but he would come walking as is his custom. Since he was about one hundred fifty feet away, I would have time to shoot him. He would run only when he clearly identified a prey. Since I was motionless, he would not see me.

If I shot him in a non-fatal spot, he would follow the faint odor of the bullet to guide his attack.

I decided to wait to see if the bears would move on. I gave this option about five minutes. It would soon be dark and in the dark, I would have no options.

The big bear decided otherwise.

Sniffing the air, he decided to come in my direction. He took about five steps and stopped again.

I decided to let out a very strong piercing whistle. The kind with the fingers in your mouth. One that was strong enough to hurt your ears.

I let the rifle rest on the branch, cocked and still pointing toward the direction of the bear.

I took a chance and tried the whistle. I thought that because it was so strong and sharp, it would echo a lot into the forest.

The whistle was a sharp, deafening shriek that echoed all over the valley. It confused the female bear. She stopped poking my things and followed the male who ran in front of her, but he ran with little enthusiasm. He knew how to be omnipotent, and I believe the alpha male in the area. I think this extremely shrill whistle would bother a bear who has hearing that is among the most sensitive on the planet.

They disappeared into the bushes, into the forest.

I had no more time. I had to go to the camp while I could see. Night was coming very soon. The clouds in the sky had misled me in time. The presence of the clouds brought the dark down much faster.

I let two more whistles echo through the woods. Then I decided to go down. I put on my boots without looking. I looked around for a second. Then leaving the chainsaw and the timber I went to the to my camp.

I say surely that carelessness is the enemy of survival in the woods. Panic would be disastrous, but it is always necessary to be cautious. Cautious does not kill.

I knew that from the moment they ran into the woods, I would at most be studied at some distance, for this fact was new to them and certainly had stunned the instinctive neurons of these two bears.

My whistling was new to them. I do not know if anyone had this previous experience, but what I wanted was to get the bear's attention and to know what they would do.

I had anticipated three reactions.

The first would be to be totally ignored. In which case they would have continued to turn the "camp" over to find food. They had already done most of that.

The second would be to be bothered by my presence. That was not something I thought would happen.

The third one where they ran away seemed more unlikely. They had the smell of food right under their noses, and I was up wind from them.

I could have tried to frighten them with the crack of my rifle. But this time I did not use this method.

But I instinctively knew these bears would be waiting for my carelessness! I had no doubt that I was a hunt for them. A strange hunt for sure, but bears were all around they were studying me and the hungrier they got, the more I would be an appetizing meal for them.

My reasoning was very fast at this moment. The adrenaline present and the exact awareness of the situation were part of the experience that a hunter acquires.

Every moment one lives is unique. Similar experiences, experienced by either one's own or another's, make you calm about how to act at times like these.

A hunter that does not have in his baggage several meetings and more dangerous hunts or bears could not experience an adventure as I have undertaken.

For the charms, emotions, and unusual situations in a singular adventure like this, a dream of the few or the crazy ones as some people tell me, is that we should have the responsibility to only do it after having enough experience, knowledge, self-control, and discernment.

I do not know precisely how many hunts I've done in my life, but I've done eleven bear hunts before, where this is the twelfth is not specifically a hunt for the bears, but perhaps the one with more bear encounters.

I studied a lot about bears. I have listened to many testimonials from fellow hunters, from friends like Loshi, the Eskimo who took me to the hunt for the musk ox, and who had numerous experiences with grizzly bears.

On my first hunt in the Rocky Mountains in the province of British Columbia, we had several encounters and learnings with our hunting guide Chris. We found at least a dozen grizzlies and one in specific. We were born again.

I came back to the present and calmly set the fire, forming a second fire, taking care to make a protection of stone around it, not only to facilitate the burning of the fire, but also that the wind did not carry a spark that could cause a fire in the woods.

I cleaned up all the mess, retrieved the pan that was bitten and pierced by powerful jaws. I could still take advantage of the pot because the hole was on the edge of the pot. This was a warning that from now on I had to keep the pots and pans out of the reach of these beasts.

I cooked a pasta with champignon sauce, which I wiped with my finger to the bottom of the pan. The hunger in the woods is incredible. Allied to physical activity and movement, the air, the environment is extremely healthy and inviting any normal human being to become a voracious lion like eater.

I write again under the glare of the fire, and although the wind is stronger, the night was not so cold. This is not a sign of bad weather, I thought.

I went to my bunker. Tonight, there were neither stars nor northern lights or anything more than the strange silence of nature.

I thought that it would probably rain at night, so I lashed a tarp over the logs that surrounded my tent. It would let wind in and out in the event of a storm. The canvas was just another protection, because I had a small but very good and waterproof tent that I brought especially for this adventure. I had tested it under a heavy summer rain in the backyard of my house. It passed with flying colors.

Sleep came and stayed with me until I woke to the steady beat of raindrops.

Manfred Zepf

Diary Day 7

A cold and Moose-less day

It was already dawn when silent, but very heavy rain fell from the sky. I could hear the rain knocking on the top canvas and the smell of rain immediately flooded the air. Now the humidity was total.

I was not surprised! The bears were not visiting me tonight.

Pools of water flooded around me making me sure the ground I had chosen to make the lodge was approved. It looked like the lodge was to be on an island.

The humidity accompanied by the cold wind made me stay for a few more hours inside my tent.

I was hungry.

Already impatient with the persistent rain that did not stop, I put on my poncho, that for several trips had always served me so well that my companions made jokes. They said that it weighed a lot and needed a donkey to carry such a heavy load. But on such a day it provided warmth and comfort

Arctic Adventure

A rope tied between two pines now served as a ridge for a canvas to form a small shed, I tied the ends so that the water did not build up in the canvas. This would let me work rather than lay around waiting for the rain to end.

I could work under my tarp making the notches on the ends of each log. These allowed one log to lock into the other.

I went to get firewood to light a fire to make some coffee. I had covered a reasonable supply of firewood.

Have you thought about lighting a fire with wet wood?

I made some coffee and drank a nice warm cup. Then it came to me that my supply of meat was zero. I decided to do some paddling to see if I could find a moose.

I grabbed my rifle, wrapped it in a waterproof case, and headed for my inflatable canoe. It was almost entirely filled by water. After tipping out all the water, I headed north.

With my binoculars, I would be able to see the moose before it could become conscious of my presence. I glided up the lake and passed the spot where crows had spotted the carcass of the previously killed moose. They made a big scene when they saw me.

This is not very good when you are hunting. Every animal in the forest watches the crows to learn when something abnormal or dangerous is happening. They are the signal to stay alert. The crows quieted as I paddled behind the cliffs.

I continued until I reached the northern edge of the lake where on my arrival with Bill, I had seen a creek that ran between the two lakes.

In spite, of the insistent rain, a thermos of hot coffee beside me and the expectation of a hunt encouraged me to try my luck in this large lake that I was sure provided an abundant of underwater and land meadow pastures for moose.

Fish jumped when frightened when the paddle with which I propelled my canoe touched the rocky bottom. The on-coming current indicated that there was still significant melting in the mountains. The lake of the "Headdress" as I had baptized it had no other way out. The only connection to another lake was this one, and the flow of the stream indicated that the level of the larger lake was still rising. This was not just due to the rainfall.

What a land!

The land was grass covered as far I could see. New green tufts at its base revealed the rapid renewal cycle in the short Arctic summertime. It is interesting to note that all forms of nature renew and grow in these six months of "warmth".

Pine trees, for example, grow a fraction of an inch each season, content to stagnate their growth completely while the rigorous winter is present.

Bears hibernate and live off the fat they accumulated during the summer.

Animals with horns lose their beautiful antlers.

During the cold of winter, fauna does not breed and little moves.

Deer dig with their hooves looking for branches and grasses submerged in the snow.

Wolves hunt for prey to survive.

All the plants and animals face the difficulties of survival.

Rivers and lakes have little movement of water under the ice. Fish seem to be asleep and make little progress in growth.

Only large movement can be observed by temperature and avalanche indicators. These are common in this region. Avalanches often move gigantic masses of snow. They sometimes take with them part of forests and secular pines, like the one that, at the moment, I observed.

Avalanches are both an amazing and frightening spectacle that results in fear for those who are near and is fatal to those who are in the way. Avalanches open a new opportunity for renewal for fauna and flora. They are wonders that do not go unnoticed for those who live with nature.

Arctic Adventure

Love and respect complement the inclusion of a way of life that is necessary for the natural balance of our existence, our spirituality.

This spectacle on rainy days has its shape altered and renewed, for even if everything remains in its place, nature presents itself in a new setting, damp, dyed gray and in every shade of green.

Behold, with a few more paddles, I had a spectacular view of a gigantic lake, I could not see the banks at the opposite end. The mountains that surrounded it, indicated to me that perhaps the lake might turn and continue.

The rain dropping from the clouds and the wind blowing particles of water from the crests of the waves that it formed in this deep lake created an extraordinary sight. How amazing it is to observe the agile arms of nature handling these elements.

With my binoculars I scoured all the banks, the clearings in the expectation of seeing the largest of the deer. The place was extremely suitable for grazing and only the moose was absent from this scenery.

I spent a few more hours going up the lake until I decided it was time to return.

"No moose today," I thought. "I'm hungry and the coffee is at the end."

It was a nice feeling to be back in "my" lake. In so few days, it already had a certain familiarity. I passed the cliff where I was greeted by the startled crows. A few more paddles and I arrived at the edge of the camp.

As I stepped out of the canoe and walked leisurely toward the camp, I came upon an irony of fate. A couple of moose ran off into the forest. They must have heard some noise I made. I did not even have time to take the rifle out of its "case". This made me sure, that today was not my day to hunt.

There was no point in going after the moose, for when they gallop out, they do not stop very soon. Going after them would surely be a waste of time.

In resignation, I took my reel and went fishing for my lunch.

With my lunch prepared, I sat down to savor a delicious fish, that allied with hunger, became a precious delicacy. I opened a can of guava. This is an indispensable treat when camping.

Putting on my cape again I went to get logs by the edge of the lake and drag them to the to the work area to make the notches. It seemed they were much heavier, and so I decided to drag them with a rope. I tied a rope to one end and with the rope around my waist I took them one by one to the work area.

To prevent getting blisters, I put on my gloves. I went through several notches without creating any blister. Since I had to make over a hundred notches to make the cabin, this had been a concern.

I notched logs for the rest of the afternoon.

Then had another serving of pike for dinner.

Finally, I took my exhausted body and went to sleep.

It was a cold and rainy night.

Diary Day 8:

Partridges and a Moose

Day dawned with a thin rain and icy wind.

I thought, with this temperature close to thirty-two, it's going to snow.

After a quick breakfast I went back to making notches until lunchtime. Blows of axes just like rowing the canoe, turns my normal appetite into "a lion's appetite" and I did not want to eat fish today. I opened a can of bean stew and ate a whole pot of rice.

"I'll take a nap," I thought. So, I jumped into my sleeping bag and slept. I woke up listening to the beating of a partridge's wings. It was already dark and no longer raining.

Arctic Adventure

And now, how am I going to hunt a partridge? With the caliber of my rifle, if I shot it, there would not be much left of the partridge. But I did not bring my sling shot either, or my bow and arrow. This I thought was an error!

How could I not remember this possibility? "What I would have to do now would be to aim at the bird's head to secure my dinner," I concluded.

I walked slowly toward the noise it produced with its flapping wings. It is like the starting a two-stroke diesel engine, that is used in fishing canoes off the Brazilian coast. It is a loud, growing noise until it suddenly ceases. It is the courtship that it makes to the attract the female when it is mating season.

I located it easily and leaned on a "pine tree" to get a clear shot. I immediately plucked it on the spot while waiting for the location of another partridge. The partridge is a small bird, so it would be necessary to have two for a hearty dinner for this hungry "wolf". I reached my goal after a few minutes of walking.

I decided to go back to camp before it got dark. I remembered Lairton, my previous partner in a Canadian hunt would always ask, "Manfred, how do you know that is the way back to camp? We did not come from this direction!" And I would respond to him, that we had made many turns in the pursuit of the partridge, but that the way back is this way.

It has always been like that. I could not say why I was sure of the way back. I had never entered this part of the forest. As I turned a full circle, the pine trees all looked similar. When I was among friends, I always joked that I had an organic dysfunction, and that I had a compass inside my head. If I were here, without such an ability, I would carefully break branches of the pines or tie-on colored ribbons to guarantee my return.

The light purple tones coloring the clouds on the horizon foreshadowed a cold night but sunny day tomorrow. I dug a hole in the stony soil so that rainwater could drain away from the fire pit. I then piled up the coals and supplied firewood and a few logs and lit the fire.

I dug a hole in the fire pit and put hot coals in the bottom. I seasoned the partridges with olive oil, salt, garlic and oregano and a little lime concentrate. I wrapped each partridge in aluminum foil and put them on the embers in the hole. Then I covered them with more embers and sealed the hole with some dirt.

I then sliced some potatoes and fried them along with some sliced onion. It was a "banquet for the gods".

After dinner, unspoken, inspired, or maybe even intuitively, I grabbed my flashlight that has excellent focus and with the "crab" I fixed it on my rifle. The crab is a wooden contraption like a mini winch that has two grooves, one that is fixed on the barrel of the rifle and the other in the body of the flashlight. With my 30-06 on board, I paddled my canoe northward.

Only a small part of the bank could be seen in the dark night. Paddling in Indian fashion, in total silence I would shine the light toward the bank in hopes of spotting a moose.

I reached the link leading to the upper lake and my expectation increased as I approached the great lake. There were many possibilities. When I first saw the area, I saw excellent sites for the pasture of this huge quadruped. Slowly and without a sound, I put the paddle down into the bedrock of this "creek."

The "hunter" whether on the ground or in the water knows the great importance of absolute silence when approaching the entrance to a lake like this. I pushed the canoe ashore and shined my light to look around to look for any sign of the moose. There was nothing for the moment.

So, I looked to my right side. I saw nothing in the vicinity. Nothing on the bank either. I turned off the light and silently paddled along the right side of the lake for a few more minutes and then, "splash."

As soon as I looked, I was scared. I saw a pair of eyes that moved quickly upward, and then at a certain height came to a stop. Separated eyes glowing in the dark night, made my heart pound to the point I thought that even the small bugs could even hear it. The adrenaline reached its limit.

"It is him! It can only be a moose," I thought.

I quickly turned off the flashlight. I approached along the bank, to take advantage of the natural full sagebrush camouflage of the lake bank. So, I went until I was very close to where I had spotted the animal. Silently, I took my rifle and pointed it in the direction of the "little eyes". I turned the flashlight on and nothing! He was not in this spot. I paddle a little more and repeat the operation. Nothing again.

Had he seen me or maybe heard some noise? Was today the day of the hunt itself?

I decided to be quiet without moving and I listened.

Five eternal minutes passed then I heard a slight movement in the middle of the "sagebrush". When it sounded like it was right in front of me, I turned on the flashlight.

It is a young moose. And it was a male! He walked about ten feet from the bank, stopped, and turned. I took off the safety and aimed at the center of his head. I fired and he fell limp. He dropped immediately. What a thrill I have when I can hunt an animal in such conditions.

"Patience is judicious," Loshi said the last time I hunted with him.

I went to the shore and walked quickly to the moose. It would be a struggle to process this moose. I was glad it was close to the shore.

With my machete I cut the low branches of pine trees. Because they were not in contact with the ground, they were dry and great for making a rapid fire.

First, I made a stone border so that the fire would not spread. I lit a small candle with my waterproof matches and used some twigs to light the fire. The fire very quickly spreads through the small pile of branches. I retrieved my candle before it melted.

I started to process the moose. I skinned it and cut it into sections. I took all the meat from one hind quarter and paddled for the camp.

I was sweating like a rain spout in a rainstorm!

Entering the small lake, an idea occurred to me: I would safeguard this moose by hanging it from the "Headdress" cliff. It would be close to the camp. It would prevent the bears that greeted me at my camp from having access. It would only be a short distance, and only accessible by canoe.

It would also make it easier for me to handle the moose meat and to unload it. The only disadvantage was that every day I would have to travel a small distance to the meat.

That's exactly what I decided. I went to the camp, left my sweaty coat, put my thick canvas travel bags into the canoe, took some ropes and sheaves and went the "Headdress Cliff".

I left the canoe on the beach and followed the trail I made a few days earlier to the point where I had strategically thrown pines down into the lake. I tied three ropes to the trees and threw them down into the lake.

I returned cautiously to the canoe. I knew I was a favorite food of wolves and bears.

I paddled the canoe over to the ropes.

I hung the two canvas bags with the rope around the bag so the bag would not hang from the straps. I lined the bag with plastic and put the boneless moose meat into the bag. This first load almost filled one bag.

Then I went back for another load of moose meat.

It was an indescribably beautiful scene as the glow of the bonfire reflected on the lake. The place was a movie setting.

I arrived with care and landed with my rifle in hand. I faced the exposed moose carcass. I fed the bonfire again and boned the other hindquarter. I chose to take enough time to set the ribs aside as well. I felt this was a risk worth taking.

It meant taking more weight on this second trip. But it would allow me to try to take the rest of the moose on the next canoe trip.

The moon began to dawn in the east and added more beauty to this scenario. When I got to the passage between the two lakes, I let the rapids take me, and they took my thoughts as well.

"God, what a place this is!

I lost track of time as I took in the lake scene. I wanted to absorb and perpetuate this beauty. It was a dream that I did not want to leave. I paddled on slowly.

I filled the first bag completely. In the second bag there was enough space for ribs.

I again turned the prow of the canoe toward the North Lake. I was now paddling by moonlight. I arrived and the fire was almost extinguished. I shined my light from the canoe towards the location of the moose. Two large eyes shocked me, and a lot of small eyes reflected at the same time. I knew it was not a bear because there were many small eyes and bears usually have at most two cubs.

From the silence of the gliding canoe, I was able to enjoy this beautiful but dangerous family scene. I paddled silently backward so that I would not reach the shore. At a safe distance I shined my flashlight. There were six wolves that were probably about two months old. It was a beautiful spectacle. I decided that I had all the moose meat that I needed. They were welcome to the rest of my moose. I had more than enough for my stay at "The Indian Headdress Lake"

I was happy that the wolf family would be well fed for a while. I did not see other wolves around the female wolf and its young, but I believed they were not alone.

So, ended another wonderful day with emotions and more emotions.

That's when I remembered: the crows! Paddling back to the camp, I thought about improving the protection of the meat bags so the crows would not feel too comfortable and feast on my meat stock. If I did not protect the canvas bag from the crows, they would be able to pierce the thick canvas and get to the meat.

I wished I could have brought some pieces of the moose and let crows have it. This would complete the arctic cycle.

I figured the night was giving me some safety time because crows do not fly at night.

"Yes," speaking to myself, "the appeal of the moose on the edge of the lake, and the volume of flesh, leather, etc., should be more attractive than the bagged flesh, that would have only a small fragrance of the flesh.

The bears ripped and destroyed the single thick canvas I used to protect the moose meat I had earlier put into the trees. Now I would have to find another solution.

I thought of creating a distraction that would draw the ravens and they would not attack my improvised meat locker. The next day I would take the bones, the hide, and remaining head to a nearby spot so that wolves and bears would be drawn by their odor and distract them from my meat storage.

The hanging meat was situated two feet above the lake. No swimming bear could reach it. On the other hand, standing in my canoe I would have easy access.

I paddled back to the camp.

When I arrived, I searched the surroundings with the flashlight. I used one eye to look for bears and another for the bath that I had to take before going to the camp.

It was already dawn and I was exhausted. I did not light the fire. I drank a glass of powdered milk, and then brushed my teeth.

Totally exhausted, I immediately fell asleep.

Diary Day 9:

A Bonfire of Beauty and Emotion

I woke up at daylight dying of cold because the temperature was at thirty degrees, and frost had settled on the open areas.

When I went to get some water for my morning coffee, I noticed that I was very lucky, because the canoe was covered with blood. It was a strong attraction for the "Ursus Horribilis". It was a big mistake to not have washed it at dawn when I returned.

I drank my coffee but paid much more attention to the surroundings than usual. My clothes, my boots, the canoe all had a lot of exposure to the moose, its meat and blood. My camp was one large attraction for bears.

As soon as I finished my coffee, I took all my clothes to the lake and gave everything a good scrubbing. I hung them far from the lake's bank in the stumps that were the anchorages of the hydroplane.

With my 30-06, I took my canoe to the site of the downed moose. I had left my knife, machete, and a plastic tarp there.

Arctic Adventure

The crows had abandoned the bones at the spot of the first moose. "They have moved on and have probably found another dead moose or dead animal," I thought.

I passed through the smoothly flowing rapids connecting the two lakes with no difficulty. As I paddled, I noticed a faint smoke along the banks of the beautiful pine forest. I figured that there should still be some burning ember in the fire ring.

Yes, the crows gave their signal as they flew to all sides. They had found their next meal. Their seemed to be about a half dozen of them. Some may have moved into the woods.

The scene at the site where I shot the second moose was very different from the night before. There were no eyes staring into the light.

In the daylight everything was easier.

I hoped not to find any wolves or bears.

And it was just that. I took extreme care as if I were going into the eye of a violent and cruel hurricane.

I saw my knife, stuck in the pine as I had left it, but my machete was about five meters from where I had left it. It was totally clean. It was probably licked by one of the wolves. The leather cover of my machete was harder to find. I found it some distance away from the fire area with many small fine bites most likely made by one of the wolf cubs. The plastic trap was almost clean, and it had about fifty bite marks.

With the machete I cut the remaining ribs to carry and throw on the Headdress area location. There was almost no meat on the ribs.

I felt watched, and I was relieved when I was back in the canoe and out in the lake.

I arrived at the Headdress beach, and very carefully, I climbed to the top. I took only my rifle and checked the whole area before I took the ribs up.

Bears have the habit of carrying off the bones and meat to avoid confrontations with their competitors. I bound the ribs to a tree so that the ribs could not be taken.

I went back to the canoe and decided to wash the canoe and clean it up as far from the camp as possible.

I took a wad of fungi and put sand on it and washed it thoroughly.

Finally, I paddled the canoe to my meat depot and took out a nice piece to make a delicious grilled meal.

Then I paddled back to the camp. I was going to eat grilled meat, hmm, I was salivating.

I was alert when I arrived at the camp and even though I saw nothing, a shiver ran down my spine. Suddenly a guttural sound of a bear came out from behind my bunker. The high-pitched "roar" was the danger alert that had commanded her two cubs to climb into the nearest pine.

The mother bear immediately rushed toward the me as it tried to intimidate me, and to gain time for her cubs to climb higher. The young cubs had small limbs, but their claws left impressive marks in the tree trunk.

Mama Ursa came toward me and stopped about ten feet from the lake. I remained out at least another forty feet from the bank in my canoe.

Immediately, even before reaching for my rifle, I paddled the canoe and slowly moved it to the center of the lake.

I felt safe at this distance. She remained on the bank watching me. It was clear she was not going to come into water after me.

The grizzly bear, as well as his white cousin, are fine swimmers. I have never known, read, or seen any documentary about a bear attacking its prey in deep water. I have seen and heard, about successful attacks that have occurred on the banks of lakes or rivers, when a hunter has been careless. The grizzly can only attack with his paws in shallow water where it is supported by the river or lakebed.

I cannot say the same of, its cousin, the polar bear, who attacks by jumping and diving from the banks of icebergs or banks. They do not even fear the deep ocean.

I would like to be a wizard and know what exactly was going on in the mind of this grizzly. She starred steadily at me like the light beam from a lighthouse. It would be fascinating to know her thoughts.

After a few minutes, she turned and let out another howl, that was answered several times by the two cubs, but they did not move down from the top of the pine tree.

I remained alert for the whole time and I kept my rifle with the safety off on my lap.

I thought about what to do to get her to leave. I only wanted to scare her. I did not want to shoot. I feared using my loud shrill whistle thinking it would confuse her and only delay the descent of the cubs.

I knew that the mother would only call them down if they were no longer in danger. I paddled about sixty feet farther away from her. I hoped that she would understand that I was not threatening her cubs, but she did nothing.

She alternately began to look at her cubs and the "lake monster," as though she were in any danger and she did not send the cubs down.

At no time did she move her foot from where she stood. It seemed that she was assessing the unusual situation of this encounter with some strange and new creature that she had never seen before. She must have been instinctively questioning the safety of the cubs and the danger of an attack on her from the unknown creature.

At this safe distance, where an attack was totally improbable, she must simply be contemplating what the family's reaction would be. For another ten minutes or so nothing changed. Then without the slightest trace of fear or worry, she walked through the camp.

The cubs remained at the top of the pine tree. They began to howl and were surely at the limit of their strength. One came down a few meters and complained giving a grunt that I interpreted as: "I cannot take more mother," and began to slowly "slip" slowly down the tree.

Mama Ursa gave a guttural roar and the one that was already slipping descended in a speed that I did not believe.

The second descended a little and stopped for a while and so on until when the first reached the ground, the mother's loud howling must have scared it because it instantly disappeared.

After another maternal call, the last one quickly descended and as soon as it touched the ground, the second "cub" disappeared in the same direction as its sibling.

It was then that the mother left in a slow run following the direction of the cubs. She did not turn back to look at me again.

There, I thought. They will not be back for now.

What a mess they had made. They had time to turn everything around. They dug trying to get under the logs of my bunker. But the provisions were safe from the sharp claws of the bears in my ever firm and strong "cage."

I lit the fire, put some potatoes to cook, cut some onions and fried them in the fat of the moose. I seasoned a moose steak with herbs and pepper and roasted it on the grill.

Wow, what a wonderous smell! I wondered if I was inviting any of my close friends to a feast on a banquet. I remained very attentive.

It had been a good day that ended in a feast! I missed the taste of a glass of red wine. I had a single bottle, but I was saving it for a later time. Perhaps, I would taste it when I finished the bunker.

Since I am not made of iron, I decided to take a well-deserved nap for an hour in the bunker. Then I would go and wash the pots and pans.

After getting up and cleaning everything, I began to drag the notched logs to the place of the future cabin. To make it easier, I pulled two at a time, as if I were in an old boat race. This made it easier, since the drag generated by the thinner part of the log decreased the drag.

With the hoe and shovel I dug into the ground so that the first log was at least half a meter below the ground level of the bunker in a groove in the rocks. The floor elevation had already passed the extreme rain test by remaining above the water and the natural drainage through the stone would prevent the wood from rotting. My goal was to give the bunker a good foundation.

The logs were green, about twenty-four inches thick part, and a little less at the other end. They were heavy. They were so heavy that I needed my ropes and pulleys to drag them into position. It would have been impossible to position the logs without a strong pine lever and a crowbar.

I did not know and could not even guess the right point at which the first log would fall into the trench. It went in without me knowing how it would land.

I worked the rest of the afternoon to level the first logs so I could place the rest. I did the front and back and then the ends. I made sure to have the exact front to back span and then I began to set the interlaced logs.

I remained alert and kept looking around. I was watching for unexpected visitors. I was now listening to dusk, I heard distant and almost imperceptible howls of wolves. They were probably with the remains of the last moose.

I wanted to take a quick look at the condition of my meat bags. I decided to stretch my trip to the "woods of the wolves", as I had baptized the place where I had shot the second moose.

Before going, I took advantage that the water at the edge of the lake was still bearable and I took a quick bath.

The day had been a cold day accompanied by a constant breeze from the west. I figured the night temperature would reach thirty-two degrees Fahrenheit.

With the temperature dropping, in addition to my Weatherby, I took my jacket, because I figured my paddling would not be enough to keep me warm.

I arrived on the hill of the Headdress and was happy to see the sacks holding the meat were intact and that the meat was cold as if it were in a refrigerator. It would take a very cold night for the meat to freeze. If it did not freeze, I would have to get it out of the bags to allow them to freeze.

I thought that I would open the bags on the way back so the meat could cool down completely. Early in the morning I would return before the ravens to close the sacks and I would tie a tarpaulin over the bags, so the sun did not warm up my "meat locker."

I headed toward the larger lake and "woods of the wolves", for I was sure they were there. The howls were constant and growing stronger.

"I will have minutes, no more than half an hour of good light to enjoy the wolves," I thought.

I got a surprise when I got there.

Two Bears were in a contest each attacking one side of the moose. Suddenly the larger one gave up what it was eating and attacked some wolves that until that moment I had not seen.

They ran away from the claws of the bear, but in seconds they came back to create psychological pressure on the bear.

On returning to the moose the larger bear did something that caused the smaller bear to run. One of the more daring wolves made a try for the carcass. When the big bear went after the wolf. The smaller bear returned to the moose. The wolves howled and meanwhile the larger bear threatened the smaller one. It did not seem very scared and continued to eat.

Were it not for the arrival of more and more daring wolves the bears would have enjoyed a banquet. Three wolves advanced to within a few paces from the banquet. Then the two bears seemed to decide to run the wolves away. I wondered if the bears could talk to each other.

I believe that the smaller either because it was full or perhaps because it did not want to fight with a pack of wolves did not return.

The big bear, who by its size must have been ten to twelve years, was now surrounded by many howling wolves. I counted eight, but there were more on the way as more distant howling indicated.

My god, I thought, there's going to be a war. The wolves began to circle the old bear. Three of them approached and growled at the bear.

"What's the bear going to do now," I wondered?

He stopped eating and set off after the three wolves. They faced him with bared teeth but stayed out of the reach of the bear's claws.

While the bear faced the three wolves, a great number of wolves had taken possession of the moose.

It was impossible for the bear to return to the moose. It would have been a brutal confrontation had it chosen to face the whole pack. It did not run, in panic, but it left in a slight jog.

The three wolves returned to the pack.

Arctic Adventure

I've never seen such a scene before. The howls of the wolves were impressive, but howls and growls in a clash, it was best to stay away from these beasts.

Wolves, how agile, I saw them from the side, as they ran. They are very agile and easily able to jump and leap. It would be impossible to face one without a weapon. Imagine being surrounded by a pack!

I watched for another twenty minutes as the wolves took turns eating, without a fight. There was clearly an existing hierarchy and the three that had faced the bear were at the top.

I turned and paddled back to the Headdress to beat the nightfall. The sky was an impressive metallic blue and there were no clouds in the sky. The cold was making its presence felt as my fingers began to ache. I hurried to the meat sacks, rapidly opened them, and then went quickly to the camp.

Everything was very calm. Nothing was disturbed. I could see nothing, there were no signs of wolf eyes or of bears. I relaxed and started the fire.

Warmed by the reactivated fire, I made a hot chocolate and took time to write in my diary. I recorded what I had seen, what I had felt, what I had experienced. It was a day I label a bonfire of beauty and emotion.

This habit of writing everyday made me know exactly what day it was, and so guided me on the timing to finish the cabin.

Today was the ninth day.

Manfred Zepf

Diary Day 10

Of Tripods and Pulleys

It was breath taking cold when I woke up. Last night I had been certain that it was going to be cold, but it was twenty-three degrees Fahrenheit. The cold was clearing the day, and I thought that even the bears would not move today.

When I got to the canoe, I took in the ice along the bank. There was ice around the canoe and out toward the banks. I knocked the ice off the oar so I could paddle to my meat locker to close my bags. Besides the rifle, I always carried a knife and a machete.

I arrived at the Headdress Ridge, and despite the cold, my curiosity took me to where I had tied the moose skeleton to a tree to entertain the crows. I wanted to misdirect those animals that watch the crow, away from my meat lockers that hung out over the water.

Tying the bones to the tree had not worked. The bears had gnawed at the rope and were able to drag all the bones away. My idea of entertaining crows and bears at this place was a flop.

In my reaction to the cold, I had forgotten to bring the tarpaulin that I had intended to use to shield the bags from the sun. I folded the ends of the bags, so they met each other. This would serve to reduce the impact of the warming rays of the sun.

I tied branches over the bags to perfectly cover them. I felt great as I closed the bags and found the meat completely frozen. If the temperature remained cold as it usually did at this time of year, I would have frozen meat until my departure.

I spent the rest of the day working on building my cabin. Using some rope and six poles, I made two four-meter-high tripods. I put one pulley at the top and one at the bottom hooked to the log. This cut the weight of each end in half and made it possible for me to raise the logs to the desired height. This allowed me to move log after log into place.

It took me a lot of time with the first log. I began using the chainsaw to cut a "V" on the ends of the log as I lifted it. The V was necessary to link the ends together and allow the logs to rest on top of each other. Envision a pioneer's log cabin. Even with my newer technology, working alone I only raised the wall by nine logs. This made the wall almost three feet in height. I planned to spend the next day on the wall that would have the door. That wall would have the only door. At the end of the that wall there would be a channel cut into a thick twelve-inch pine to hold the logs.

Lunch was a pasta with mushroom that I had brought in dried form but was quickly softened in the hot pasta water. I accompanied the lunch with delicious water from "Headdress Lake".

Dinner I decided would be a repeat of the same menu.

Later in the afternoon, I felt that I had a good day but felt that I needed accelerate my work.

Diary Day 11

World of Super Reality

The following morning, I attacked the cabin very early. I was very eager and feeling extremely happy. At each fit, the logs received a huge nail. This immediately gave the wall rigidity.

It was a beautiful day of sunshine, with a light breeze but it was quite cold in the shade. I made great progress. I had time to work on making some trestles. I cut dry pine into slices. Some of these boards would later serve a totally different purpose. I cut the boards from dry pine, because when cut from a green pine, they would not have had the same strength and as they dried, they would probably twisted out of shape.

For lunch, without great culinary pretensions, I opened a can of black beans and put them on the leftover rice that I had already cooked.

Afterwards, I returned to building the bunker.

A few more prepared and placed logs later I decide to stop for the day.

I went with the canoe and went to retrieve a frozen piece of moose.

I returned to the camp and decided to take advantage of the forty-eight-degree Fahrenheit heat wave and got into the lake for a bath before the cold returned.

Arctic Adventure

It was always hard to get in. I sometimes jumped in and other times took a dive in and at other times I went in slowly. Today courage was missing, and I entered the water slowly. Once the water got to my waist I fell forward and began swimming. I tried to get warm by swimming. I stayed on top where the water was warmer. I was careful not to get a cramp and I stayed close to shore. I spent almost three minutes in the water! Even under these conditions, I felt good after a bath.

I was fondly remembering taking showers when I was young when suddenly, from somewhere above, I heard the well-known sound of geese! On the horizon there was a formation of at least a hundred geese flying at a height indicating that they were not intending to land nearby. They flew right over the Headdress Lake toward the north. It is interesting that they fly thousands of miles with their compass always marking the course of the North Pole, until they find the exact region where they have been returning for years.

"Impressive," I thought.

I got out of the lake and was about ready to dry myself and return to camp when I saw a huge bear. It was walking through the camp, smelling everything. It was the biggest I've seen in my life. I quickly picked up my rifle, my companion that I always carried at my side, my clothes, and a towel, and I slowly went to the canoe.

The huge bear was more than fifty meters from me but if he attacked, I would not stand a chance. If I were to shoot, I would have to accurately shoot him in the head to immediately immobilize him.

I was moving. It had not yet seen me. I knew I was in an extremely dangerous situation.

I was shaking with cold. I was barefoot. I had no clothes on! I did not know if I would die of cold or the attack of this giant.

I had to decide quickly, before he saw me, between taking a very precise head shot or get to the boat that was a few meters away.

I decided on getting to the boat. I was extremely careful to make no noise or any sudden movement. I wanted to take advantage of the bear's myopia. I quietly but as fast as possible, put my clothes into the canoe. I knew that time was both vital and decisive.

It seemed an eternity from the moment I carefully unhooked the boat from the rocks, lifted the bow, pushed it forward and out into the lake far enough where I felt safe. I crouched and without sight of the beast, I took a few steps into the water until the boat was out deep enough and would take my weight without dragging the bottom on the stones and thus producing noise.

Seated in the canoe I did not have sight of the bear. This meant that he would not see me until I had reached the center of the lake.

In moments I was out of his reach.

If I had made any noise while on shore, the bear with its keen hearing would have reacted to a noise that was different than the normal forest noises of falling branches or other moving animals.

I was at the center of the lake and he had not noticed my presence. I was downwind from him and he could not pick up on my scent. I knew that by not making a sound and getting out in the lake I did not have to directly face him or try for a kill shot or possibly be attacked when he charged.

With the oar in my hand, I faced in the direction of the bear. I did not want to lose sight of the bear. I saw him and could not help but be impressed by its monstrous size. I wished I had my camera in my hands to register it. At a safe distance, I watched his movements. I still had not been noticed.

The bear as I have said is myopic, and if we do not make a sudden move, it has difficulty locating us by sight. In cases like this it is wise to always keep cool, because if you know a little of how the bear acts, you have a better chance of surviving.

However, with his hearing and smell, he will not be fooled. The bear can smell the man's presence a few miles away if he is downwind from you. This time, by my luck, the wind saved me.

I whistled loudly as the bear tried to attack my stockpile with his claws. He stopped immediately he was confused by the strange noise that now echoed through the woods. I watched as for perhaps twenty seconds the bear stopped, put his front paws on top of my temporary accommodation as if to gain a better observation angle. It then returned to his initial purpose.

Arctic Adventure

I gave a second whistle, as loud as I could. I wanted to know if whistling was a way to keep bears away. I thought that perhaps because of the extreme sensitivity of their ears, it would bother them. The result this time was frustrating. The bear paused for a few seconds, gave an unobtrusive look around without rising as he had the previous time, then returned to his action. I gave three long whistles in a row, and yes, he promptly located me in the middle of the lake and looked at me. Watching him with my riflescope, I studied his reaction.

He had located me. He kept his eyes on me. What would his reaction be?

I stared at my rifle, while now leaning on the oar, trying to imagine what was going on in the bear's head. What would it be thinking of that strange being that was certainly the cause of the hisses he had heard? What I wondered was going on in the head of the one who was the supreme being of the whole continent. Nothing intimidated him. He was omnipotent. He feared nothing, he was not being attacked by anyone.

How would he deal with something strange, with a sound he did not know? But he certainly did not know fear. Curiosity probably kept him staring at me. He did not leave the camp, nor did he react to me. Turning again toward my camp goods, he returned to his attempt to reach food. The food was different and unknown, but apparently tremendously appealing.

I did not rest and did not give up trying to reach him. Even with the adrenaline rush, the chill the cold breeze produced on my wet naked body was making my teeth chatter. I had sat exposed for quite a while without taking much notice, but the cold had no pity. I dressed quickly without even drying myself, always looking at what the bear was going to destroy or do. I knew I would have some more time before nightfall and decided to be patient and see.

I would have a unique chance to observe this monstrous bear trying to break the resistance of the protection which I thought was exaggerated when I built the bunker but at that moment it seemed to be somewhat fragile compared to the size of the bear.

He clutched my boots, sniffed, and kicked them away. The bear probably did not like the smell!

The bear went to the kitchen and I thought, "not again". I thought it was going to knock over the protection as it stood and took in the smell of fried fish and meat fried onto the grill. To my surprise, he knocked over pots, bit the grill and licked it so much that I would not have to scrub it. With his weight he kneaded the pan previously bitten by another bear.

Then he walked to the cabin, sniffed everything, turned to the chainsaw, and was evidently bothered by the smell of gasoline. He did not bite it. There must have been some annoyance with the strong smell of gasoline.

He returned to my bunker and made attempts to enter from all sides. I was pleased with his lack of success since that was where food, clothing, gas, everything was stored.

The bear managed to pull the closing log and succeeded to open the top entrance. I had forgotten to tie one end of it when I went to get a moose steak.

This absent-mindedness could no longer exist.

"If it happened without me being at the camp it would cost me dearly," I thought.

And now? Seeing that he found a "hole", he was sure he could enter.

Oh no, oh my!!!

So, when he was preparing to enter, I aimed at a huge stone next to the bear and shot a warning to him.

This time it worked.

The bear acted out in a rampage, pawing in a dreadful way, and left huge paw marks on the ground.

Then with astonishing speed it fled into the woods.

I was worried that it would be dark before long. Luckily, nightfall held off. Without a light in this bear's habitat, I was literally in a distressing situation.

When I got back to shore, I checked the grooves left by his mortal and sharp nails, of which a single swipe would have annihilated me. If they left marks in such a way on the ground, in the logs, what would they do in humans, or in animals?

Arctic Adventure

The bear is an exceptionally dangerous animal, sublime and incredibly ferocious. It looks like a docile stuffed animal, and at the same time it is the most voracious beast on the planet.

The feeling of being able to be here, in this moment, at this time, in this place, with all those sensations of being here provided me extraordinary feelings and depth about this adventure.

Having survived, the cold and its sensations, I now found that I needed to come back from the world of super reality, to warm myself by the fire and to feed my body.

Manfred Zepf

Diary Day 12:

Good Memories and Cowboy songs

I woke up with my nose aching from the cold and red enough to brighten my day. I did not need to go out to look at the thermometer to know it was cold.

Even the bears do not like it when it's this cold. They did not show up on the cold nights.

I rose and went to check the embers of and revive the fire. I then prepared some hot chocolate.

I began to lay the cabin logs to warm up. The worst part was preparing the logs to fit. Afraid that I would run out of gas for the chainsaw, I decided to make the notches with the ax. I would need the chainsaw to cut boards.

Arctic Adventure

Today when I stopped for lunch, I wanted to eat a northern pike. I cast the artificial bait and with a single strike, I lost the bait. I was sure that the grandfather pike of the lake had hit my line. On the next cast I hooked one that turned out to be about two and a half kilograms. It would be my lunch. I cooked some potato fries to go with the pike.

I was methodically looking around for bears. I wondered if the bear visitor of the previous day had brought any other friends from some other region.

By the afternoon, the cabin walls had reached more than six feet in height and I needed to redo the scaffolding.

At dusk I lit two bonfires with a lot of wood to discourage the return of any unexpected dinner visitors, especially the giant one from the day before.

Dinner was to be a delicious Canadian/Brazilian barbecue of coarse salt rubbed moose meat.

I remembered my "little brother", Conrado, who had demonstrated his barbecuing mastery in numerable previous international hunts. He made the most memorable of the barbecues I've ever eaten in a hunt.

This was a hunt in the heart of the old American West, outside of Gillette, Wyoming, USA. The barbeque was prepared on the farm of James, an authentic cowboy friend.

He prepared the barbecue before the curious eyes of the cowboys. They were astonished by how different the preparations for the barbecue were.

Conrado was not using ready-made charcoal, or charcoal lighter. Nor was he using a normal barbecue stand. He was not using the ready-made supermarket barbecue sauce.

Instead, he dug a one-meter pit. He surrounded it with a brick border and made a bed of wood.

He then prepared the cuts of pronghorn meat that we had hunted that day with salt that we had brought from Brazil.

Bringing in the salt with us from Brazil was an unusual enough story. When entering the United States, the customs inspector in Chicago thought the coarse salt was cocaine. He finally believed us that it was only salt after we put some in our mouth and declared that it was only salt.

Conrado declared, "It is only salt! Then he asked the agent to try it. He explained it would be used to make Brazilian fashion barbecue." "Notice that we have also brought some skewers to hold the meat on which we will put the salt."

Guardedly the agent took a piece and tasted the coarse salt.

"Wow, how salty," he exclaimed!

"Of course, it's salty, its salt!" I exclaimed in Portuguese. This caused our travel partners to burst into laughter.

"What," asked the distrustful prosecutor because of so many laughs?

"Yeah, it's salty because salt is salty, right," my cousin said in English!

Once again, we laughed, now accompanied by a half-embarrassed laugh from the agent. He was not totally convinced of the charm of the joke.

The same curiosity had been staged by James, a legitimate cowboy, who experienced the coarse salt also exclaiming it being very salty.

Patiently, after shielding the pieces of salted meat from the wind Conrado placed it into the barbecue.

The cowboy was again curious about the "Brazilian fashion" of barbecue. He mentioned it was too early for dinner and he would not be hungry for several hours.

Conrado replied that it would take at least that long for the meat to be ready.

From time to time, Conrado patiently turned the skewers and the aroma that emanated from the barbecue pit provoked our appetites.

As we sat around the grill pit, James, wearing a bandana and cowboy hat, took out his guitar and accompanied by his wife and little boy, sang Ian Tyson songs. It made all of us feel the unique and wonderful panorama of the west. We all sat under the same sky and looked much like a scene from the last century.

Arctic Adventure

Then later my brother used a knife to knock the excess salt off the meat and served us the most memorable of barbecues.

It was an extremely tasty, succulent meat and the barbeque was talked about so much in the small town that the people came out and wanted to know the secret of how to make "Brazilian Barbecue".

The memory was wonderful, but it was time for me to return to the present. I looked carefully around for any unwanted visitors. Then I enjoyed the great, Canadian/Brazilian, barbeque of salted moose meat that I had prepared.

I climbed into my bunker and fell asleep staring at the stars in an extremely dark and still night.

It seemed that as soon as I fell asleep, the sound of the teapot being knocked over woke me. Half asleep, I remembered having left my unwashed teapot in which I had heated my chocolate.

The teapot was my alarm, and it let me know that my visitors were in the makeshift kitchen. I could not see them because the fire had burned out. I got the flashlight. I knew they were in the kitchen because they were making a lot of noise.

I wondered if I was being visited by the first bears that had visited me. I noticed that it was four eyes and not two that looked into the light. The bears were very close together. Were there two cubs? Or were they two adults, a male and a female?

I turned off the flashlight once I determined they were not making much of a mess. I wondered what I should do.

I then saw their silhouettes against the faint fire embers. They were very close together. I decided to try a sharp whistle but waited until they came closer. If they were not intimidated by the whistle, I would try to scare them with, as the Indians used to say, my "fire stick,"

Very shortly after they passed me, they came sniffing back toward me. And they were both sniffing for me. I felt a connection with the actions of the two bears. Understanding the bear's motives greatly reduces the adrenaline rush one feels when being surprised by their appearance and actions.

They were not afraid, and they are bold and hungry. The dark of night seemed to increase the size of the two bears. The shadows made by the fire reinforced the feeling.

One bear climbed up and was sniffing at the entrance log I used to get in. The other poked his muzzle through the logs.

It was time, I thought. With both fingers I gave the strong whistle. The one poking his snout in, jumped back, and ran out into the forest. The second bear at the entrance log had a different reaction. He jumped down a few feet and stopped.

I heard the first gallop and the second descent, but I thought they were no longer there. When I pointed my flashlight in that direction, I saw one was, standing on his hind legs. He was watching but a few seconds later, he followed in the direction taken by the first bear.

I climbed out with my flashlight. I knew that I could be detected by my movement. I did not want to be surprised the way it had happened a few days ago.

Who was the male, and who was the female? I would never have the answer.

Which bear freaked out? Which one fearlessly rose to face the unknown?

The whistle had probably been successful because of the very short distance to the sensitive eardrums of the bear. Was it for this reason that the second bear had gone a little longer to face perhaps a different situation? On the previous day when I whistled at the larger bear from a good distance, he practically ignored me?

I would probably have other opportunities to try to decipher this puzzle.

"I'll try to get in touch with some scholar or someone who has a lot of experience with bears," I thought.

Diary Day 13:

An Absence of Guests and the Hoot of an Owl

The next day, I woke up to the wild cries of crows.

They brought me back to the reality of the Northwest Territories. There they were taking flight flaunting and announcing to the whole forest that something different was happening. I took the canoe and went to the hill of the headdress to check out the situation.

Yes, it was time to see if my meat lockers made of canvas bags were intact. They were, but I added some more branches to protect the bags from sun and certainly also from all the crows. I was worried because at the top there were no more meat or bones.

Because the ribs I had tied to a tree no longer existed, I would be susceptible to an attack. And I figured the attackers would be either wolves or bears.

I went up on the hill, I looked with binoculars and I did not see or feel anything different.

I wondered if the crows could smell the frozen meat. I checked the meat lockers again. But if the meat was tightly closed and frozen, it should not spread any scent. How strong was the smell of these crows? I concluded that Yes, the crow must be like the vulture, but the vulture smells carrion. Surely it was amazing the crows were at the location of the meat locker.

I opened the one bag and took out a whole piece of rump. It was very large but my hunger after handling logs always increased my appetite. As the meat was frozen and would stay that way for a few days it was the ideal amount, so I rowed back to the camp.

I prepared the piece with coarse salt and put it in the brazier.

Then I went to work placing heavy logs.

The smell was torturing me. How would the bears react when they identified this true "banquet perfume"?

I knew that the wind carried the scent over the lake. I understood I could have visitors, so I had my rifle properly positioned beside me.

Lunchtime had not even arrived and Humm, the aroma of a barbecue treat was overwhelming.

I finally succumbed to the aroma and enjoyed a wonderful meal.

I finished by enjoying a delicious guava.

The absence of unwanted guests was somewhat surreal. Though wolves howled nearby, I knew they were not so bold and would not likely appear.

It was unbelievable that in twelve days, the wall logs had reached the nine-foot level. I had done more than I imagined. Now it was time to make the door and windows. I would have loved to make them broad and open as we in Brazil thought windows should be. But I thought with the mind and eyes of an Inuit and needed to make a window that would prevent a bear from entering.

Small windows would let me enjoy the dark and I needed my sleep.

I did not want to be surprised anymore. I would need to know of an approach from the back of the cabin.

Tomorrow I would set up a rope with all the well-washed cans of powdered milk, baked beans, and corn at a two-and-a-half-foot height. The bear would want to go under, and its passing would rattle the cans and sound my "alarm".

I sat on my canvas chair, enjoyed the cozy bonfires, refreshed myself by eating the meat left over from lunch and then I read until the wee hours.

An owl flew over, landed on the pine, and let out its hoot. This lifted my attention from the book.

I wondered whether there was a deeper meaning.

I remembered the story about the great Chief Sitting Bull, of the Sioux also known as the Dakota. Their enemy also often called them the Crow which meant creep like a snake. He had been resting in the shade of a tree when a woodpecker warned him, "do not move, do not move. The big bear is coming but lie down without moving and he will not hurt you."

A group of nearby Indians saw the huge bear sniffing and circling him. They did not know what to do as they watched in astonishment. Then the huge bear sniffed around Sitting Bull, ignored him, and went on its way. Sitting Bull recounted the woodpecker's warning, and the story became broadly known throughout the tribe.

Sitting Bull was responsible for the ritual called "ghost dance or spirits dance." He never hunted birds again and came to understand the omens and their signs.

There seem to be so many situations within this natural world where the Indians seem perfectly integrated. They bring to us so many memories of remarkable experiences that it is impossible to remember all of them.

Hooting from time to time, the owl suddenly took to the air. Just as it had come it fluttered away and vanished into the darkness.

With the hot chocolate gone, the weakening bonfire's light hypnotized me into thinking of sleep as I bade farewell to the owl.

The crackling of the fire made me certain that nothing would bother me, and that the world could not be any better.

It was time for me to sleep.

I lay down and sleep immediately overpowered me.

Diary Day 14

A Waterfall from the Sky

I woke up to the ever-negative chill of dawn. I slept very well. I ate my usual breakfast to accompany me along with usual cold.

I noticed that it was time to redo my stock of firewood. I did not have to work hard to get firewood in abundance near the camp. With the ax I went to the "Bear Avenue" and cut an old dead pine tree, among the many, fallen by a strong Arctic storm. It would have the chance to give service one more time.

I set the bear alarm along the back of the cabin as planned. There were three well-divided sections. If a bear passed under the rope, the noise would be very high because I arranged it so the bear rubbed the line it would cause the cans to rattle. I fenced almost fifty yards. This would help but it was no guarantee.

Once the alarm was done, I finished the fitting a pine log with a four-inch groove to hold the logs of the front wall. This log would be the left part of the frame for the door. I prepared a similar log for the other side and prepared the top and bottom of each to accommodate a cross member of the same thickness. The frame and a heavy door would be a bear stop.

I planned to put in window, but I did not have an idea on how to make them, but I prepared the logs for them.

For lunch I reheated the meat and added pasta with tomato sauce. The chef did wonders with the food.

Afterwards, I went to assemble the logs that would be the support of the roof's ridge.

They formed triangles. One end of the triangle would be on the front wall and the other end on the back wall.

Since there were no more heavy logs to lift, I no longer used the tripods with pulleys. That was a mistake, because I needed a lot more strength and strained my body more than on other days. I was extremely tired at the end of the day.

I had a chocolate, but I did not want to have dinner.

The wind started to blow a lot that night. I was worried because wind increased every minute and began the churning of my alarm bells. Surely it was not caused by bears, and they might even be frightened by this noise.

I fell asleep but when I woke up, I had a pain in my back that was most probably due to the weight of the logs and coupled with sleeping in a bad position.

I decided that I would do lighter work for the day.

I could not make my coffee. The wind was too strong. I thought about making a little fire inside the cabin. But I decided it was dangerous to stay in a corner of the cabin with the fire and expose myself to the bears.

I worked to make the notch of the ridge when I saw a torrential rain closing the entire horizon.

I quickly grabbed my rifle, wrapped the chainsaw in a tarpaulin. I then I quickly covered the bunker. I tied only one side and left the other side loose with ropes so that after entering bunker I could tie the ropes inside.

I went in and tied the inside ropes as the raging rain poured down like a waterfall. There was no lightning, no thunder but a rain that surpassed any that I could remember experiencing before.

I jumped into my tent and closed it because there were streams of rain everywhere. I was happy to be sheltered in the tent. Everything around me was drenched. It rained all morning. With back pain and the furious rain outside, I lie quietly and read until the lyrics mingled and I fell asleep.

It was great to have slept. When I awoke it was four o'clock in the afternoon. I did not want to do anything. I had read and rested in the hope that I could do something today but that would be impossible.

I thought snow was going to fall because the temperature was dropping steeply. I got wet enough under the improvised canvas. I got some crackers and drips of water caught by a pan provided me plenty to drink.

Since I could only think of catching pneumonia if I went out into the cold, I decided to read. Then when the wind and rain let up the temperature dropped. The day did not improve enough for me to continue working on the cabin.

I put on my poncho, went to the bathroom, brushed my teeth, and went back to the warmth of my tent and sleeping bag and slept all night.

Diary Day 15

Two Bears and a Ridge Pole

Some noises woke me. Two bears were looking at me! Yes, a medium-sized bear and a larger and taller one. The bigger one climbed to the top of the bunker and stared down at me.

Instinctively I took paranoid action. I filled my mouth with air, and I made that sound of escaping air, waved my hands, and then loudly shouted, Boo. The mad rush towards the woods of the smaller bear scared me! It was so scared that it is probably still running to this day. I felt powerful! The larger one just slowly descended from the top and lumbered away.

I gave a sigh of relief.

It was now time for me to get up and get to work.

It was a very wet, cold, gray day. A strong, constant wind blew in random circles that kept me from being able to move in a normal manner.

After a quick breakfast, I decided to attack the cabin roof ridge so I could put on the roof planks and cover the cabin.

Then I would make the door.

Only then would I be able to work in peace inside the cabin.

The task at hand was to raise the ridge log that would support the whole roof structure. Using rope and pulleys I raised the heavy log into place. I had selected this log for its strength and size. The ridge log and the cabin walls would hold the weight of the half logs that would be placed from the ridge log to the wall.

The first layer of half logs would be placed flat side down, next to each other. A second set of half logs would be placed flat side up in the groove made by the first layer.

Then a series of plank would run across the roof from end to end covering the half logs.

Finally, a bark shingle layer would cover the planks.

The ridge and the entire roof were difficult tasks for one person to tackle. It took half the day just to get the ridge log in place. I was pleased to have been able to do it by myself, but it was almost more than I could handle.

I stood and looked up at the ridge log once it was in place. It was a feeling of relief and gave me a great feeling of accomplishment.

The day was loaded with hard work. Except for almost slipping early in the morning there was little excitement. A slip and fall from the wall might have ended my dream. But thank God, I was able to hold on and prevent the fall.

The day went rapidly by and finally it was time to break and prepare dinner.

I was too tired to be a distinguished North Canadian "chef".

I ended the day with a simple meal and retired for the night.

Manfred Zepf

Diary Day 16:

The Rice Pot and the Squirrels

I woke to squirrels attacking and fighting over my rice pot. I had left the rice in a pan to use for my upcoming lunch. Squirrels!!! Always the squirrels. They had decided to attack the pot. They knocked over the pan when my presence scared them.

I decided to let them have the rice. It would be fun to watch them. Initially two squirrels returned for the rice. There was one big one that I took to be the male. He would take the rice in his mouth and carry it toward his hole. Then the smaller one that I took to be a female arrived. She did the same thing but went in the opposite direction.

Another larger squirrel that I took to be the female alpha squirrel arrived and then squirrels kept arriving until I lost count. But none of the squirrels took any rice because they were vying for position.

The large male returned but he could not drive the others away. It was a bad situation for all the squirrels. I had food for everyone, but it seemed that would not happen.

I figured if I distributed the rice there would be a share for each of the squirrels. I made six mounds far enough apart to let them all get some rice.

I made my coffee and drank it and realized that I had run out of eggs. I had planned to have eggs for fifteen days and as planned I now had none. I should have planned for more!

I went to work on the roof and soon thought that lunch would taste great.

When I came back to the kitchen to prepare pasta for lunch, I saw that everything with the squirrels was still the same. The big male squirrel ran from pile to pile and would not let any of the other squirrels near the rice. This was not what I had intended. I spread the hills farther apart to a radius of fifty meters. Then it was a squirrel party. The large male squirrel would charge one pile and the other squirrels would take rice from the unguarded piles and carry it away. They cleaned out the rice and the large male squirrel ended up getting nothing. For me it was ironic that the big powerful bully was left with nothing!

It seemed so right.

I went fishing for my lunch. I had a wonderful place to fish where the quarrelsome, gleaming golden-scaled northern pike, jumped relentlessly out of the water making a wonderful spectacle to behold.

The tremendous force when a pike hits the lure always made it seem to be a much larger fish than it usually turned out to be. However, this day I thought for sure the line would break. Just when I thought I was bringing it in, the pike would shoot out with a force and power that was more than any fish I had so far caught.

Almost all my line had played out before it began to tire. It took almost ten more minutes to bring him slowly in. He was so large I was afraid to raise him out of the water by the hook. I decided to pull it through the water to the beach.

The pike was big and wide and probably six kilograms in weight. It was too big to eat in one meal. I would have fish for days to come. I could not let him go since he was exhausted and would probably die.

I thought about fish bones and that the ones in this northern pike should be very large and easy to take out. I also thought about how wonderful it would taste.

I thought about the situation. If I let him go in the water, he would die. The other fish would devour him. Leave him on land and bears, wolves, crows, would take care of him. I was convinced that keeping him myself and enjoying the wonderful taste was the best choice.

The "chef" in me made me take the time to properly clean and prepare him.

The hunter in me made sure that I disposed of the scales and insides by throwing it out into the lake.

Then the hungry laborer in me sat down to enjoy the fruits of his labor.

I really enjoyed the taste of the fish. As I ate lunch, I was watched by a day owl, and noisy birds. The light wind completed a wonderful lunch scene.

I spent the rest of the afternoon between sawing, nailing, and trimming.

It was late in the day and I had a strange, uneasy feeling. I looked toward the cabin, checked the bear alarm sensors which were rattled by the wind, but I saw nothing.

I ate a part of the fish and washed it down with clear lake water. Then it was time to get ready for the night.

The uneasy feeling only subsided when I decided it was time to go to sleep.

I got into the bunker, secured the entrance while still thinking something strange was in the air.

I went to sleep earlier than usual. As soon as I lay down, I was asleep.

I lay down and I fell asleep quickly.

Diary Day 17

A Dream of Legend

I had an amazing dream. When I woke up, I could not help but wonder about the meaning of the dream world.

I immediately picked up my pen and began to write down all the details. I wanted to capture my dream before I forgot any of it.

In my dream, I was at the edge of a pine forest on the edge of a very high rock and a mighty river ran below.

I saw a village in the lush green valley formed by the river. Plumes of steam were rising from Indian teepees indicating that meals were being prepared inside. I seemed to know the place and the people.

I came down from the rock and mounted my horse.

I rode my horse out into the valley and I greeted them by name.

"Good afternoon Tatanka! I respectfully greeted him. Where is Crazy Horse? I've brought your order," I exclaimed, as I dismounted from my mount.

"He's hunting, but he'll be here before the cloak of evening comes," he replied quietly as he invited me in.

I greeted Tatanka's parents. They served me a few pieces of smoked buffalo.

"Your white friend has been here three moons ago. He is always with Crazy Horse to torment him with hunts," Tatanka told me.

No sooner had I settled in when some horses galloped up accompanied with tremendous shouting.

It was Crazy Horse with his hunter friends! He and Gray Cloud descended from their beautiful animals. They came, straight to their tents.

We embraced each other as good friends. Before he could say anything, I congratulated him on his successful buffalo hunt. There was a nearby buffalo herd and Crazy Horse prided himself on his ability in being successful.

"Am I going to be able to hunt with you again," he asked enthusiastically?"

"Yes, Crazy Horse and I brought some boxes of ammunition for you," I replied.

When I removed the ammunition from my horse's saddlebags, Crazy Horse said loudly, as he held up the ammunition, "I have to hunt until the great white robe is gone and the green of spring returns."

"Yes, and before the next winter I'll be back and I'll bring you more ammunition," I told him.

"Will you stay here until the next hunt?" his face turned to that of a mischievous boy as he spoke with an imposing bearing.

"Yes, I will hunt with you." I replied again.

Then I woke up to the North Canadian morning.

At the moment I awoke, I came two centuries forward towards the present.

It was disorienting.

What an incredible thing!

I could not stop writing this dream down. It was as clear as it was intriguing, with names that made history of a life of dignity and struggle for their people. They exemplified loyalty, justice, and wisdom far beyond what most people could understand or live.

Was the owl a messenger of the dream or a coincidence? My feelings of longing were inexplicable. They had taken possession of my spirit. It was a situation so familiar to me that it seemed real.

I was transported to a dream world of abstract realities and yet, it was so striking and familiar that it seemed to be real. I could not describe what I felt at my return to reality. It was a mix of homesickness. They were feelings that confused my ability to interpret them. There was a sense of collaboration between friends.

What I is the meaning of this dream, I asked myself.

I stumbled over the spit of the barbecue as I walked out of my bunker.

A squirrel had pulled it from the grill, I ran after him causing him to climb up the first tree he found. I was shooting great photos with my camera.

I got the fire started and made my coffee. After a coffee with powdered milk and toast, I went work on the construction of my future cabin.

I worked relentlessly. I wanted to see my cabin ready.

The chainsaw did an incredible job of cutting the dry logs in half to make the roof. Finally, it was time to put on the roof.

The bears had not visited me in the last two days as I made the notches, raised logs, pounded nails. Perhaps all the noise had kept them at bay.

I was alone but did not miss the visit of my northern visitors.

I wondered what I might dream on this night.

Diary Day 18

Tranquility

I woke up wonderfully rested, and with a sense that paradise exists here on earth. I tried to identify why I had a delicious sensation all these days. But today this feeling was markedly greater! I felt a peace enveloping me, which was a balm to my spirit. I became so overwhelmed. I listened to the birds singing. I looked out to the lake. I absorbed the beauty of the majestic pines while the breeze was caressing my face with a luxurious scent of pines and wildflowers.

Oh my God, what a peace.

I relived the moments from my arrival and choosing this location as a base for this adventure. I remained intoxicated with this feeling. I did not even bother to make a breakfast. I think I got the needed energy from the tranquility of the moment.

What it seems to me, I concluded, is that the human being forgot to interact with nature, to feel enveloped, to seek this peace that I felt now. I can say that every day that have I lived here I have felt the beauty that God provided. I have spent hours in this reassuring balm. I wished the feeling of this moment to be eternal.

I have worked with music all my life. It has given me a sense of accomplishment. Hundreds of live concerts have given me many moments of pleasure. I was able to enhance the singing of good musicians.

I felt the pleasure of enhancing the live performance and presentation of musicians using my mixing console and sound effects. Through hundreds of controls, I had the power to further enhance the performance and presentation.

This ability is very, very rewarding.

A good sound engineer can improve the performance of a band with not-so-good musicians, just as a bad sound engineer can worsen the performance of a very good band. I had the victory of the moment. I love what I do, it's adrenaline in the veins that shivers the skin when the live concert begins.

And that is the feeling I felt now. Yes, it's very, very different. I would say that it is an introspective journey, in a magical moment without influence of anything besides God.

I came back to the world around me to find one of the squirrels in my boot. It brought me still more joy. She had decided to check out what it was.

I got up to share a meal with her. She was scared to see that I, who had been sitting frozen in thought, moved. She raced immediately back to the protection of the forest.

I resolved that even with all the peace that had enveloped me, I would have to dedicate myself to the construction of the cabin. It was a harmonious part of this paradise. It would be a corner where I would be in peace whenever I returned.

I did not have lunch and not much desire to make great efforts. I studied how to make each notch and how to lay the wood, and I finalized the design of many finishing touches that the cabin would need. I did not do much work.

Yes, today I did not work very hard.

I finished the day by taking my inflatable canoe along the banks of the lake. The light, lazy breeze did not even swing the tops of the pines. The lake was a mirror of the surrounding tranquility. Only the waves of my movement disturbed the reflection in the crystalline waters.

Like a wolf, I drank from its waters.

I then returned to the camp. The stars were my blanket, on this most striking day of my life.

Diary Day 19

Bears, Storm and Missing Canoe

It was the hottest day so far with a temperature of sixty degrees Fahrenheit. The cabin was beginning to take shape.

I had brought glass in the thought of making a small window to provide light. The four almost one-half inch thick, nine by ten-inch glass panels that I had brought were too much for a single window. I planned to make the windows single panel glass lookouts that could be closed with a board.

I had yet to cut in the windows. I would cut them in at the end of building the cabin. Until that time, the cabin was even better and safer. The thought of a window and being able to look out at the landscape gave the cabin the warmth of a home.

I still had to make some thick, strong boards for the entrance door. I was leaving this as the last task for the chainsaw.

I was in the middle of sawing logs for the roof when I decided to stop and prepare lunch.

Arctic Adventure

I was getting ready to get my fishing rod from the bunker when I heard my "bear alarm" ring. I immediately picked up my 30-06 and walked to the bunker.

I climbed slowly up to the top and I was able to jump in at the exact moment that I saw two bear cubs arriving. I tied the log to close the entrance to the bunker and I watched quietly.

I thought the two bears were already weaned, since they looked to be about two years old. They were too small to have triggered the alarm. They would not reach the height of the rope. I then looked around and was startled to see a huge bear only about five meters away walking toward me. I had not made a sound.

The bear already had my scent. She was sniffing and without blinking, she began to point her nose at the logs of the bunker. I felt like a caged bird when the cat is trying to catch it. I controlled my desire to poke at her snout. The tarp was on the outside of the bunker and the bear clawed at it as if to trying to kill it.

The two young bears knocked over the kitchen, and together they went to the cabin. In an instant they climbed up the scaffolding and ripped the canvas from the chainsaw.

Suddenly one was up on the cabin roof. It walked on the roof with an odd ease.

Meanwhile the mother was trying to get to me. The cub on the roof could not get down. The mother stopped her efforts to get into the bunker. She grunted and the cub on the roof promptly turned around and began to back down to the edge of the roof. It stopped when it was hanging by its front claws.

I think it cried for help. It howled as it hung by its claws.

What claws I thought.

Agile like a cat, it gave a start and went up on the roof again. The mother took the time to encourage the cub. I wanted to tell it to go down whenever he wanted to or not, but it was better for his mother to take care of it.

The other cub went back to attacking everything. It scattered the wood; messed up the cooking area then came over to the bunker. It was, unstoppable.

It then decided to go to the lake. It drank water and became frightened when the canoe carried by the wind, flew in his direction causing him to leave.

Good, if it had decided to bite the canoe, I would have been in bad shape.

Momma ursa outside of the bunker seemed to resent standing on the back paws trying to see the desperation of the cub on the roof.

A strange wind began, and within minutes it began to intensify. I could not imagine the outcome of this scenario. The wind suddenly seemed to help me by knocking things over, bothering the bear family. At this moment, one cub ran to its mother's side. A few seconds later it started to smell my protection cage again. The mother began to circle the cabin while the climber kept calling its mother.

The wind seemed to bother the mother bear for she looked in the opposite direction of the wind. She seemed apprehensive. She made her way into the cabin, at that moment a pine rafter fell on her side, I was not quite sure if it hit her. She did not go crazy.

I noticed the darkening roiled sky overhead. A huge storm was building on the horizon.

The bear seemed to sense it before me. She concluded the visit with a howl, telling the cubs that she was leaving. The wind was so strong that it lifted her hair and made it stand straight up. After her last howl, the climber on the roof decided to descend. It hung from the edge and fell and ran into the woods. This was a sign that nothing happened in the fall. It was in a hurry to catch up to the family.

I thought, yes God is taking care of me, because I always end up not having to shoot any bear. It would not feel good to shoot down a mother, or even a male. I knew I had invaded their space.

Very quickly the tranquility of several days of sun gave way to a formation dark thick nimbus cumulus clouds that in less than twenty minutes turned the day into dusk. The wind suddenly rose into a fierce summer storm. The wind broke the remarkable silence that existed in this end of the world.

The wind howled like dozens of wolves and became so strong that it took the pots and pans, knocked down the logs and sticks that were leaning against the cabin.

I ran after the pots and gathered them in.

Arctic Adventure

The wind was beginning to carry branches and boughs of pine trees in its gusts. It was bending the trees into frightening curved ways.

I quickly went to the lake to get a bottle of water and noticed that the waves were cresting and breaking heavily on the shore of the lake. The water in my bottle was a little cloudy, but I did not care. It was all made up of natural elements.

I returned to the camp and quickly covered the chainsaw with the remainder of the canvas and fastened it tightly, so it would not fly, as everything else was doing at that very moment.

The fury of the wind seemed to be mercilessly trying to mow down the pines. With large nearby trees being battered, I thought it wise to get into my protective bunker. It now seemed to be too small and too fragile for a tall pine tree to fall on it.

The day became dark. Deafening thunder accompanied by blinding lightening seemed to herald the end of the world.

It was two o'clock in the afternoon.

Nearby pine trees fell as if they were nothing. They confirmed that this was one of the famous storms that come from the north and bring destruction and cold. These are feared storms that come from the North Pole.

It was a spectacle that I would remember for all my life. With hundreds of hunts in various corners of the planet, I had never seen anything like this before.

At the same time that we feel totally helpless, we observe in wonder this action of nature that transforms the landscape and secular settings.

I was impressed by all this, but when thick raindrops began to fall, I retreated into my tent. I thought the rain was getting heavier, but they produced audible noise only in tiny intervals between the thunder that was almost continuous.

Big hail stones now reached through the logs to my tent. I worried, that they could rip the nylon.

Half an hour of persistent storm left a totally different scenario from that which I had left when I entered my shelter.

The ground was, totally covered by a layer of hail. Many trees were toppled. The temperature had dropped to almost zero degrees centigrade.

I was impressed.

I wondered what had happened to my canoe. When I got to the lake, I was scared. Where was my canoe? I had left it tied on the bank out of the water. Was the wind so strong that it threw it back into the lake?

The sky remained overcast. The day was now a terribly humid cold that was aggravated by the strong and constant Arctic wind. I slipped on my rubber boots and ventured along the bank of the lake to find the whereabouts of my canoe. I took comical tumbles on that ice mixed with gravel and smooth stones.

Even using my binoculars, I did not see the canoe anywhere on the banks of the lake.

I the rest of the day would be devoted to finding my canoe. Walking on a slippery layer of ice I went around the lake. I had my rifle as usual. I assumed the canoe had been blown away by the wind. And the wind was blowing northwest. But I saw nothing in that direction.

I concluded that I would have to go around the lake. I went in the direction that the wind should have blown it. I found nothing.

I walked among the grass that was in shallow lake waters, for more than two hours looking and found nothing.

A short distance away, I saw a pine that the wind had overturned and thrown over the others. It was caught between other pines well above the ground. If I went up there, I would certainly have a better angle of view of the lake. I climbed up and crawled out to the pine.

I reached a height that I felt might be fatal if I fell. But I was desperate to find my canoe.

As soon as I sat down and balanced myself, I began to search. I tried the left bank, the right bank and saw nothing. I tried to see the lake shore better with the binoculars.

Arctic Adventure

I was about to give up. I could not imagine it having sunk or to have gone in some direction against the wind. And it could not remain lost.

I had to find it.

After nearly a quarter of an hour of searching, I saw a spot in the middle of the grass along the edge of the lake. I examined the spot carefully, and yes it could be the canoe or a tree trunk or a stone. But looking hard through the binoculars I was almost sure it was the canoe. If it really was the canoe, it would almost be impossible to get to it because it was in the middle of very tall grass and tree limbs.

Even though I had seen it, I did not know how to mark the exact spot where I was on the lake bank. I had no exact reference on a distance of two hundred meters.

The pines along the bank all looked the same. I counted out two hundred steps and with the machete cut my way through the brush and I went searching. Then ahead, partially submerged, trapped in some tree limbs was the canoe. Its location explained why it was not easily found.

I turned over the canoe to get the water out. It did not sink because it was inflatable, but the storm had filled it with water. And the oar made of wood would float but it was gone.

The disappearance of the oar was a very alarming detail. Without an oar I was screwed. I got into the canoe, and with the wooden stock of my rifle I began to paddle. I figured if the wind brought the canoe, the oar must have come too. I began to search the bank from side to side but saw nothing.

I gave up because I had to continue with full dedication to finish the cabin. I had only made one of the pine roof boards. I went back to the camp using the "rifle" as a paddle. I had never imagined in my life to use the rifle as a paddle.

I tied up the canoe, and prepared dinner. It was prepared from a can of black beans, some rice, and a piece of moose meat.

Afterwards I improvised a functional paddle for the canoe. It was made of a flat piece of pine and a limb tied as the handle.

I slept to the delicious smell of rain and the fragrance of pine prepared by a wind that whipped the pines to fill the air.

Diary Day 20

Fantastic Paddle and Wonderful Sleep

I woke up very early. The day was cloudy and cold. To warm up I took the "fantastic paddle" and went to retrieve some moose steaks for my meal. The "fantastic paddle" was a poor replacement. I missed the much lighter, smooth non-tiring pull of the missing one.

There were no crow alarms at all! It was early and not time either for them or for any other animal. There was no singing of birds nor did I see any. The fauna and flora knew the time to retire and resignedly waited for a better day.

Soaked by the spray that the wind picked up as the waves hit the canoe, I returned to the camp. Not even the pests of the squirrels that always stole my biscuits and food from the pots were in business.

I seasoned my moose steaks, made my coffee, and had a small piece of meat and some rice for breakfast.

I then attacked the roof because I did not want any more bears there. The marks of the climber's nail were carved deep into the structure.

I put the boards over the base rafters.

The hard work developed a huge hunger. The moose steak that I had seasoned in the morning called me to lunch.

It's the truth, I heard it call my name!

Even with dry wood, shielded from the strong wind, I could not light the cooking fire. I was reduced for lack of choice to eating the leftovers from my previous day's dinner and the now chilled iced potatoes. I concluded that hunger was the best of the cooks.

My firewood supply was low so in the afternoon I decided it was time to gather more dry wood. I went to the "Bear Avenue" to look for the wood. I never felt at home at the Bear Avenue. Now it was a "minefield" full of bear coconuts. I had to be careful to look where I stepped.

I cut the first logs with the rifle across my back. Because it was so cold, I did not anticipate any bears, but I was still stressed by the potential. I cut numerous logs and stripped them with the ax. I hastened to drag them back to camp. I did not want to linger in the "Bear Avenue". I took enough to replenish the wood pile and left with the last log.

Dinner was a cold chocolate, a dehydrated apricot and plum, accompanied by crackers. The "chef" was too tired to cook and was looking forward to sleep.

The cold was insistent and powered by the wind. The cold had the effect of making the moment of being under warm blankets and enjoying a luscious pillow, an invitation to sleep.

It was a delicious feeling, and I accepted the invitation and fell asleep.

Manfred Zepf

Diary Day 21

Mama, Papa and Baby Bear

The morning dawned sporting a thin rain but a little less cold. The wind persisted but was blowing lighter.

I decided it was time to light a fire in the protection of the cabin. I improvised an internal covered fireplace with shells as the base.

This would give me a safe warm place to make a door and prepare the windows.

Feeling good about this idea, I drank a coffee and had breakfast.

I place some logs in the doorway opening to make any bear access difficult. With my rifle inside I knew that if I had visitors, I would be trapped inside but I could continue to work.

I fried a succulent moose steak on my new hearth.

I decided to go out to get my tools from the toolbox and was surprised by the arrival of a medium sized bear. It was slowly walking toward the cabin. It was sniffing the air and was most likely attracted by the aroma of the moose steak.

I was certain it also had my scent and was aware of my presence. It had come for food and I was potentially a good dish for him. With the rifle inside my bunker, I quickly re-entered it and inserted a board between the ones that I had placed to make it difficult for a bear to enter.

Arctic Adventure

I had to think fast. The bear might want to enter the cabin because of the smell of the two steaks in the frying pan. I hoped that the steaks were more appetizing than I would be. That would be divine.

Otherwise, I would need to use my rifle to defend myself against an attack.

The bear was very close when it stopped and stared back from where it had come. Suddenly it ran off in the opposite direction.

Oh! Boy, I thought, there is probably a bigger bear coming. Carefully, I put my head out through the future door. I looked both ways. Then I put my head all the way out to see what was coming from the direction the bear had looked.

I saw a cute teddy bear!

I immediately knew, the little bear could be a huge problem. The cubs always followed their mother. The mother watches and sniffs everything in great care. The mother bear would likely be at least six or seven years old.

Yes, there she was. It was not much bigger than I. But it was certainly a female with a cub. And that was sure trouble.

I looked at the beautiful and graceful teddy bear that was only a few meters away. It was very young. It was most probably born in the spring. I was hypnotized by its grace.

I decided to throw the frying pan out with the steak in hopes that I could throw it farther. It was the best idea I had. The steak in the cabin would only act to attract the bear.

I tossed the first steak about twenty meters away. The little bear gave a bellow, a bellow similar that of a newborn calf. It ran to its mother. The mother sniffed the air and headed toward the steak.

To my surprise, the mother bear arrived after the cub had the juicy steak. When I threw the steak in that direction, the young bear must have taken the risk of taking the steak. She took the juicy well season steak and put it in her mouth and ran some distance away, as adults do, to eat. The mother took the steak and ate it in front of the desperate cub.

I did not immediately understand and thought it as an inhuman mother. Then it began to sniff and look in my direction.

I had no idea what to do. I had a bullet in the chamber and my finger on the trigger.

What to do now? I saw another bear! I thought. I'll get rid of the second steak and frying pan which continued to exude smell of the moose.

I threw the steak about the same distance as the first throw in the direction of where the bear was coming.

I tossed the frying pan out too, in the direction of the bears.

I thought I had made something happen because the mother bear gave a long, loud howl, and made the cub run. Then I panicked, for the young bear came running straight toward the cabin. It was the only thing it saw to climb into and hide. When I saw that it was going to come in, I pushed the toolbox into the door and with a board I kept the cub from entering.

The female certainly heard the howls of the young bear. It gave an alarm to the mother bear who must have gone to meet the male.

When the little bear bellowed, his mother turned and saw it running toward the bunker. She must have vetoed that action, for the cub turned and went to the nearest pine tree and climbed to the top.

It was providential, with the teddy bear up in the tree, she headed toward the young male bear. I looked to see where she was going.

I was evaluating if I could get to the bunker. The top was loose so I would be able to quickly get in.

I saw the bears start to smell. It was the ritual before mating. I wondered if she had forgotten her young cub. It was the time when the bear was supposed to be in the mating season.

I decided to walk barefoot so as not to make any noise. I exited and hid behind the cabin and peeked out. I didn't think they saw or heard me. In a straight line, it was about forty-five feet to the bunker, and I would be exposed all the way. I decided to use the camouflage that the cabin provided. I walked ten yards hidden by it and I had only five uncovered yards.

I slowly walked these five yards without taking my eyes off the two bears. I stood up slowly behind the bunker and climbed in.

Inadvertently the top log made a scraping noise that stopped the bear courtship.

The mother bear came running in my direction. I jumped down and almost fell. She ignored me and ran by toward the pine that the young cub had climbed. The cub was coming down, but it stopped when she gave a howl.

The male was coming.

He would not neglect the baby. The young cub represented a future enemy. Male bears only saw the cubs as food.

The mother was the defender, this was why mothers were listened to and feared.

The male was probably approaching because of the smell of food. He found the frying pan and licked it and bit it.

I think this encouraged him to go to the cabin. I wondered what would have happened if I was still there. Would I have had to kill him?

Now there would be nothing but the smell and the bowl. He entered the cabin through the boards I had placed across the opening, in seconds, with little difficulty.

The bowl in which I had sautéed the moose meat must have been attacked. I immediately heard it fall from the scaffold. No sooner had he entered than he was leaving.

Believing that he was going to continue mating he walked toward the female bear.

He stopped when he began to smell me.

The young cub was not holding on any longer and began to slip. Immediately the mother gave a howl, and it climbed another few feet, and began to cry.

Mom instinctively let out a howl toward the male who seemed to see that she was not playing or dating. She let out another guttural growl.

The male bear turned and ran into the woods.

Okay, I thought, now is she's going to dedicate herself to me? Will she protect the cub and keep it in the tree?

No, she passed me and ignored me and with a pleasant howl, I saw the cub come down. It was crying and complaining non-stop. It hit the ground and ran straight into the woods from where it had come. Mother followed her running cub.

I was alerted to the fact that I had to make a door that would protect me from any unexpected guests.

I had survived this scare and it was only mid-afternoon.

With some logs, I sealed the door and only had access through a board.

I decided to take the dry logs and make four-inch-thick boards. They would be ideal to withstand attempts by non-guests.

I had brought four farm gate hinges for the door. They could withstand the weight of heavily made gates almost for the rest of their lives. I had carried them and paid the airlines extra for their weight.

When Bill, saw the hinges he said that not even a bulldozer would take the hinges down. He laughed at my exaggeration. But now after multiple visits from my bear friends, I realized that the hinges were exactly what was needed.

The end of the day arrived. Tomorrow I would finish. It would take a lot of effort with the auger to make forty-eight holes, through the four-inch-thick boards.

It was a good thing that the wind subsided. I managed to light the two fires.

I cooked my seasoned moose on the fire that had been the kitchen.

I finally ate my seasoned moose steak.

Our Lady, how I ate!

Diary Day 22

The Bear Proof Door

I woke up with a different idea in my head for the door!

Sometimes we sleep with a worry or fright and strangely the next day we find a solution that seems to appear out of nothing.

I would have to work almost all day to make this door. I did not want to worry about the bears that were frequent and offensive.

First, I set up three fires in such a way that it was not dangerous for me to pass by the fire as I come and go but would be a deterrent to the approach of the brutes. I needed to keep the flames on while I worked.

This done, I could focus on the boards for the door framework. I start by supporting the vertical boards of the frame. After smoothing the planks with my handheld wood planer that I have had since I was 15, I trimmed the edges so that the gaps were minimal and came together to fit perfectly into the width of the frame.

Arctic Adventure

This door would swing open outward just as most doors in the bear regions do. I had been curious about this and asked a gentleman who lived in Churchill's Bay, why this was so. I also asked about an even more curious fact, the nails that stuck outward some four inches through the door. He explained to me that bears are curious animals. They will smell mainly on the doors and windows since there are more cracks. Bears can weigh more than seven hundred fifty kilos and when they lean on an inward totally nail free swinging door, it always collapses. The door hinges and locks of an inward swinging door always collapse. The outward swinging doors are insurmountable because they are supported by the door frame that includes a bottom brace. This requires those entering to step over it as they pass through the door, but it adds another level of support for the door. The nails sticking outward makes the door like a vertical Fakir's bed. If the bear tries to lean on the door it will feel the pain from the sharp nails and will stop.

His explanation made perfect sense to me.

I made sure the doorstop would have an extra thick three-inch frame stop.

I worked quietly. Nothing was abnormal in the camp.

I opened a can of sardines. And toasted some bread that was getting soft and losing its taste. I ate some bananas. This made up for the half-eaten lunch.

With that agony of a runner who is about to cross the finish line, I wanted to finish the door. I was determined to make this door super reinforced. I made each hole with a hand-held drill. I then put in a bolt and tightened on the nut. Finally, I bolted on the hinges. The door looked like those at the entrance of a castle. It was an absurd mass.

I was ready to mount the door. I fed the three fires to protect me before I mounted it. I wanted the protection when I turned my back to the camp while I adjusted the door. I used wedges to raise the door into place. It took me three tries. Then with a carpenter's pencil, I marked the 12 holes in the frame stop that would hold the hinges. I removed the door for the last time. I drilled the holes into the frame. I placed the hinges over their respective holes and screwed in the bolts.

The door was finally closed for the first time. It looked great and I was proud of the "castle" door.

I now worked on the inside lock. It was a lock made by a thick slab of wood with a handle that was bolted in the middle to the door. It docked in an iron-square-u-fixture mounted on the door frame and on the edge of the door.

The door closed and locked perfectly from the inside.

And on the outside, how would it open and close in a safe fashion? Oh, if I had not thought in advance, I would not have been able to find a perfect solution in the middle of the woods.

The door locked on the inside when the lever was lowered into the u fixture. It was impossible for the bear to pull the smooth door from the outside.

The simple solution was to attach a cord to the top of the locking bar, route it up and to the outside of the door. The locking bar could then be lifted from the u channel when the cord was pulled.

Then I decided on a solution that did not require the cord. This would prevent any curious bear from pulling the cord. Instead, the door could only be opened by sliding a knife, thin sheet of metal or a machete from the outside and lifting it up. This became the intriguing secret of the cabin door.

It was time to take my first bath in my cabin. I brought in my clean clothes and set up my indoor shower that I had bought at a camper's outfitting store. It consisted of a plastic bag with a shower head with valve attached to the bottom. I went to the lake and filled a bucket with lake water. I was happy to take the first shower in the warmth of my candlelight.

My first bath taken inside the cabin was delicious. Even though it was not hot water, I was out of the wind, which sometimes made taking a bath a torturous event.

I knew the cabin was not yet done, but it was time to change my address. I would sleep in the tent set up in the cabin because the roof was yet to be completed. I would have the comfort of being able to cook, sleep peacefully and bathe. I would also be able to stock fish and meat and not be afraid of the bears.

Arctic Adventure

I was clean. I was secure.

I used the last eggs and made rice with a scrambled egg for my dinner.

Tomorrow I would cook beans.

I was very happy.

The remaining work was to finish the roof.

Yes, I slept happy in my new home, but I thanked my bunker, for the safety and protection it had provided.

Manfred Zepf

Diary Day 23

Monster Bear, the Paddle, a Hungry Visitor

I woke up to a gentle breeze.

I was intrigued by crows making a racket very close to the camp. Corpses are silent. Crows make an incredible noise if there is danger. I took my rifle and headed toward the "Bear Avenue." I knew something out of the norm could have happened there. There was so many bear droppings that no animal except squirrels would venture there. And even the agile, expert jumping squirrel has often become a small dish for a bear.

I cautiously went all around the Bear Avenue. I saw a huge grizzly among the fallen pine. It was eating something, ten yards from where I had my logs.

Holy Cow! It was a monster.

I did not want to see anything else. I was sure there had been a clash between bears. One of them died. It had to be this monster that killed it. When bears face equals even the victor can die slowly from the injuries it sustains. In this case I believed that this giant had been drawn by the chatter of the crows.

Slowly with eyes wider than a chameleon, and a silent walk I returned to the camp.

I knew I had a bear that was near a world record in size and weight very near to my camp. He would not be of this size and weight if he were not the cunning alpha male in this territory.

It was hard for me, but I had to let go of my plans for the day.

In the warmth and safety of my cabin, I drank my coffee and had my breakfast of cereal, raisins, and powdered milk.

I retrieved the food box, tent, sleeping bag, clothes and kitchen supplies from my trusty bunker and carried everything to the cabin.

I had smashed all the trash to decrease the volume. It was not much, because the cans were always hung on the "alarm line" and the plastic and packaging, very little by the way, had very little volume when smashed. I kept all of it inside a thick sack, inside the food box, so the terrible squirrels would not mess it up. It would return with me on my journey back to "civilization".

The other item was gasoline.

I was now sawing the last boards to complete the already bear-proof roof and thus make it rain proof. I knew that it would have to withstand the torrential rains of the Arctic.

I dedicated myself to completing the number of boards I would need to cover the roof. I kept one eye on the chainsaw and another on the outskirts of the camp.

I only ate dried fruit for lunch.

I closed the day when I had cut the last board. I also ended with a respectable appetite.

I took the canoe to get more meat. I wanted to roast some ribs on the grill. I wanted a second piece of the rump.

I went to the Headdress Hill.

I got a little worried because the temperature had risen, and the meat might begin to thaw.

I arrived in the canoe with my homemade super-oar.

As I went close to the beach, I saw a very strong reflection on the beach exactly where I usually disembarked to go up to cut the pine trees. I thought perhaps I had forgotten something. I wondered what I could have forgotten. Perhaps some canvas or piece of plastic.

I paddled over and I was very happy to see what I had found. The right word to use would be "driftwood" because the paddle was being washed in the surf, and thanks to this movement I found and rescued it.

I did not make the exchange of paddles, and with the improvised oar I went to the meat bags. I took the meat that I had come for. I saw that the rest of the meat remained frozen.

I finished the trip using my makeshift paddle. I did not want to risk losing the paddles and took both to the cabin.

I reactivated the fire, made a ditch to make a brazier. I seasoned the ribs, wrapped them in several layers of foil and threw them on the coals. I then covered the foil with charcoal left over from old fires and then I covered it with stones. I had learned this from the Indians in Brazil. They make fish or meat wrapped in sheets of banana leaves. It's a delight. The ember below the rib, will roast without burning, and the rising heat begins to ignite the upper charcoal, roasting equally, as the stone cover traps the heat and exchange of air.

I would eat the ribs tomorrow.

Since my hunger was now immense, I decided to grill a steak for dinner.

While dinner was on the grill, I prepared to take a shower. I wanted to keep the air in the cabin and my clothes clean.

I bathed again with warm water.

I was cold because the temperature had dropped. I opened the door and took a few steps and stopped. I saw a bear. It was not close, and I could not properly assess its size. I decided not to risk it and went back into the cabin. I took up my rifle and flashlight. The bear did not leave immediately. It lumbered right over to the bonfire where I saw it and then I saw nothing. It was not there anymore. I pointed my light from left to right. I saw nothing. I turned to the side of the cabin. I immediately jumped back and locked the door. The bear was exactly fifteen feet from me at the far end of the cabin. I knew it was after the meat or me.

I was hungry and salivating.

Now a bear had come to take the meat.
"Oh no, I do not think so," went through my mind.

He had stayed around and had not taken the meat because of the fire. I could not think straight, but I picked up the frying pan and started pounding on the bottom of the pan. The noise almost made me deaf. Then in this deafened state I tried to listen to see if the bear was still around.

I opened the door and quickly threw the frying pan into the middle of the path between the bonfires. Nothing, there was no attack on the pan. I opened the door again and threw out my coat. Similarly, it was not attacked. I opened the door and stood at its edge. I used the opening movement to cautiously look out. Since the door opened outward, if the bear attacked it would push me in and close the door. I believed that it was gone since it had not attacked the pan or the coat.

It was not in front of the cabin. I went to the side where it had been, and it was not there. I thought then that it was gone. I could get the grill using the knife as a handle. With the rifle cocked, I went to the grill, and then the bear appeared. It was about sixteen feet from the right side of the cabin. Slowly I put the knife and meat back on the grill. I raised my rifle and aimed just above and between the eyes. It would be a kill shot.

I was on the verge of a heart attack. We were eye to eye, just a few feet apart. Occasionally it lowered its head and looked away. This made me wonder where to shoot. Then the bear seemed to be bothered by the light or the fire, and it went back to into the woods.

I took the steak and slowly returned to the cabin though I wanted to run or fly back. Once inside and I locked the door, breathed a sigh of relief and took a deep breath. I think the excitement and tension had been so great that I had forgotten to breathe.

I calmed myself down and I had even lost my hunger.

Finally, I sat down to eat and enjoy my steak.

I could not blame the bear for wanting the steak. In this cold it had to replenish its calories.

I flossed, brushed my teeth, and then went to sleep.

It was very cold, and the wind circulated a lot around the cabin because I had not yet caulked the cracks between the logs. This was the last of the tasks that needed to get done. I had not had the time until now to do it.

I thought of the caulk, the windows, and the bear. I did not even realize I'd slept when I heard a noise. I got the light and saw it was 3:40 a.m. and the bear was still hanging around. But I heard nothing else. It was almost dawn when I went back to sleep.

The bear, as I saw it in the early morning, had kicked the grill and sent it rolling away.

Diary Day 24

Marvelous Culinary Event and Mosquitoes

After checking out the bear's damage, I made myself some coffee.

There was not much to destroy, but he had taken the grill, and disappeared with it. I went about figuring out what the bear had done. I found the grill and to my surprise there was some flesh burned to it. He must have taken the grill as soon as the flames had died. I deduced he picked up the hot grill and burned himself then threw it away.

I thought he might have pawed the platform. I went to look where I had first seen him.

Yes, there were foot marks there.

I felt like Sherlock Holmes himself.

I went to work on the cabin, and I was soon ravenous,

Just after eleven I decided on an early lunch. I removed the still warm stones that covered the ribs.

Our Lady!

Arctic Adventure

The meat was cooked inside of the aluminum foil. The juice had no way to escape so the meat was juicy and falling off the bones. What a delight! Lunch was a marvelous culinary event. I ate so much that afterwards I needed a nap.

This was the day that I would finish sawing the roof boards that would overlap and go across parallel to the ridge. I got them all standing on the side of the house. I planned to put them in place on the following day. They were the secondary protection against rain leaking in. They would get covered with bark shell tiles that would run down counter to them and would be the primary protection from the rain.

In the evening I had a different set of visitors. I had not expected to encounter mosquitoes so far north! It was hard for me to imagine them surviving and hatching in the cold water of the lake or any other body of water so far north.

Yet they were friendly and only bit me a few times.

Manfred Zepf

Diary Day 25

The Immensity of Peace

I woke up very early, without any outside interference.

I ate my breakfast cereal and had a coffee.

After looking for a certain the absence of "Ursus Horribiless". I climbed up and began to lay the roof planks. In a short time, I finished the whole roof. Then I trimmed the roof edge at each end with the chainsaw.

With one eye on the roof and the other looking for my frequent bear visitor, I did not see the approach of what undoubtedly the most striking storm of my life. The change of intensity of the wind and a sudden silence present in the woods, served to alert me.

I looked to the North.

Yes, the "North Comes." This expression, very common among those that inhabit the Arctic and the northern Canadian provinces bordering the near arctic, means that "The" storm, from the north, is coming.

In it, the lightening is much more powerful. The thunder tremendously frightening and the accompanying wind is stronger and very violent.

The storm of the "North" really makes us remember God even more.

Arctic Adventure

I have at countless times, faced storms.

One about half a century ago was with my brother Conrado. We were riding on a road of a eucalyptus farm. With no other option than to pray and continue, we faced a storm from which there was no escape from the endless minutes of lightening, thunder and branches plummeting us from the skies.

Another terrible one was my survival on the high seas in a seventeen-meter-long fishing boat. Giant waves washed over the small boat wheelhouse as they washed from bow to stern. This was perhaps the three worst hours I've spent.

Now at this moment the gray-haired man, foretold a storm that I had never seen and delivered what he promised.

The wind carried in its fury, a strong smell of pine. For sure the leaves and branches had been whipped by this high and violent wind.

Countless and indescribable were the lightning bolts that were followed by thunderous crashes. It was as if the sky was breaking. Then after a few drops of rain, and behold, hail stones begin the bombardment, and in a few minutes made an icefield. The hail was so intense that I could not see the other side of the lake.

The noise in the cabin, under the roof, was deafening!

Protected by my heavy poncho I peeked through the open door. I watched everything. I thanked God for the tall pine trees around the nearly finished cabin. They were my natural lightning rods. For the moment they were unharmed.

Entire clumps were torn out where the channeled wind was raging through the woods that bordered the lake.

Everything calmed down after half an hour of the spectacular choreography of nature.

My cabin survived!

I walked out onto ice covered ground. There was so much ice that I could not see the ground. After two slips, on the round and slippery rocks, I arrived at the canoe. The wind had blown it out of the lake to the end of its mooring rope, but it was not damaged.

I laughed because with almost no push it slipped easily back into the lake. And then on the shore it ran into and was stopped by an accumulation of ice brought in by the wind.

I cleared the ice and pushed the canoe clear of the ice.

I thought about making the Brazilian drink, "caipirinha", by mixing ice with sugarcane liquor, lemon, and sugar. Mother nature had made her own.

What I saw, what I felt, because it was a magical moment, a page written in my life, I eternalized in the form of a poem, a song.

This immensity of peace

From this side of the sky
    Attacks the blue, huge storm.
        Suddenly everything turns to grey.
Traveler from the far pole,
    The fury of your icy rain
        Reaches to the bottom of my soul.
            The soul of the Arctic.
You cross the feelings of fantasy.
    You curve the giant pines.
        The survivor heroes.
Enduring bravery across the wide horizon
    Buttressing the wonder in this realm.
Kingdom without a crown.
    Yes, fragrant,
        Forever majestic.
You perfume all the songs and charms,
    From this forgotten and solitary world.
Oh, you are so beautiful,
    Eternal in command of the lands you sail,
        To blend,
            Water,
                Wind, and
                    Ice ...
On this side the northern storm,
    On the other side our star king.

Arctic Adventure

Majestic to travel in the evening.
    In this land of anonymous heroes
Then day by day in this great vastness
    No one, only owners of this beauty.
True to these great things,
    Rays to run the skies,
        Thunder to echo the feelings,
            Rain to wash our souls.
Everything,
    Everything touches us,
        Yes, we see everything.
            We feel it all.
Thus, the storm advances,
    To understand
        Yes, to understand.
That everything in our life comes and goes,
    To learn to appreciate every moment.
Yes, to embrace this lull that is now made.
    Ah, peace…
For the love of this land,
    Faithful to feelings.
        An everlasting gratitude for all,
            To Him.
When finally,
    From these grand and ancient pines,
        Droplets falling from their branches,
            In an attitude of respect,
                They bowed to the storm.
                And to the crying sky.
To experience such infinite peace,
    The moments
        The reflexes, and reflections of life.
A star now casts its light,
    Brightening and warming all it touches
        At this time, a different brightness
        A glow of infinite peace,
            An endless reflection from every drop.
            It casts a mountain of light.
Everything takes me to the top!!!

Manfred Zepf

Without looking at the weather,
Without listening to lies,
I just know how I think,
How much I feel,
What I love so much.
Ah, nature,
Ah, mother, how much you reveal.
You touch me deeply.
You touch my soul.
Alone in this forgotten corner of the world
You never awaken loneliness...
You refer us to ourselves,
You magnify us.
Peace reigns unbroken,
In all the details,
These are moments that smile love at us,
And that we will never forget...
This moment of silence
Interrupted in the form of a song.
By the same deep feeling,
For this eternal and magical moment.
To listen to the silence.
I stop time to reflect on peace,
The exact time of the eternal ...
I feel Him in everything,
The soft breeze caressing the sensations of the now,
The last rays of the sunset,
The tireless and beautiful star-king,
He leaves us under His blessings.
Brightening even more
This immensity,
This immensity of love
This immensity of peace...

After the storm, in the following silence, everything was brightened by the last rays of the sun.

Bark Roof Shingles

Diary Day 26

Roof Tiles

I set out to cut and strip the bark from enough twenty-inch long by six-inch diameter logs. Each log would yield two roof tiles. I was not sure how many logs I would need. I selected two long slender pine trees to begin with. I hoped they would be enough to create my "wood bark roof tiles".

Making the roof tiles would also create a good supply of firewood that would hold me for the near future.

I cut standard twenty-inch logs from the pine trees. Then I cut the log in the longitudinal direction. I then was able to take off the "bark roof tiles" with ease. I did this until I had enough tiles to cover the roof.

The pile of half logs was impressive.

This took much longer than I had anticipated.

I could not use green wood boards to make tables, benches, and shelves for they would secrete resin and grow mold. With the chainsaw that had never let me down, I now had these last tasks to complete.

The cutting of the dry pine would have to wait for a later day.

The sun going down in glorious show of color warned of the coming night. It was accompanied by the rumble of my stomach that reminded me how hungry the work had made me.

I had skipped lunch and I was too tired to do much cooking. The "Chef of the North" chose to warm a can of black beans to put on top of some leftover rice and quickly grilled a moose steak.

It was the dinner of a "King" and hunger that made the Chef a Genius.

Diary Day 27

Honey, Chocolate and Caramel

I had brought two ultra-violet resistant tarpaulins specifically to put over the roof below the bark roof tiles. I had used the tarpaulins under my sleeping bag where they had served their first useful function. Now they would be used for their primary function of ensuring the cabin roof never leaked. I attached the plastic on the roof top and was ready to put the "bark roof tiles" over it.

I pulled up the bundles of tiles. I put them on from the bottom roof eave to the roof peak. Each higher shingle overlapped the one below it. I was pleased that the shingles did not crack when I nailed them down. Perhaps it was that they were still green. Two rows of upward facing tile were then joined by one row of downward facing tile.

The roof peak would have a downward facing row across the length of the roof.

By Late in the afternoon, I saw that I had only enough tiles to cover two-thirds of the roof. My estimate of having enough tiles was a sweet deception of my mind. I had to "produce" more tiles. I got ready to go and cut another pine tree.

When I started to go down from the roof I saw, emerging through the pine trees closest to the cabin, a small bear. It looked like a big puppy. If he had not yet been weaned, I knew he would be in the care of a mother bear who would follow him closely. Just as I had the thought, the mother bear appeared. Yes, I've seen this movie before.

Momentarily distracted by my observations and thoughts, I realized that the bear smelled me and had identified my direction. I had been going up and down countless times carrying up the bark tiles and I had left my rifle down on my semi-finished table.

Ironically, the first place the little bear went was to the table. At first it sniffed my gun. Then to my good luck, the tea pot diverted its sniffing attention. There again was my sturdy, fragrant teapot about to have another experience with bears. In an attempt by the bear to lick inside, the teapot fell to the ground.

The different noises produced in the fall of the tea pot frightened the cub. Momentarily my rifle was safe from being overturned by the great cub's curiosity.

Bears always smell, paw, drag, and dig everything. The mother, distracted by her cub's mischief, located me at the exact moment I was raising the ladder. In no hurry after looking at me, she circled the cabin, now sniffing the gaps, now sniffing my way.

I knew I was safe on the roof. If she ventured to climb the roof it would be the time to act. I would hit her paws with my hammer. I waited to see what her attitude would be. She tried the door. It was closed. She tried to push, and pull, but she was not able to get in.

I did not want to waste any more time with them. My rifle was in danger of falling. It had survived a bear kick already, and I did not want to take another chance at losing it.

The mother bear certainly did not find me an easy or appetizing prey. She was slowly moving away from the cabin. I was no more than twenty feet away from her eardrums. I gave a sharp whistle that shattered the silence. She jumped off the ground, released a guttural sound to warn the cub of danger. The cub shot up the first pine tree available. It was the identical action that all cubs take, no matter their size.

The little one climbed the height of the pine with the speed of a cat. It demonstrated a keen capability of missing the limbs on the way up. The branches of the ascending path seemed not to exist.

The mother bear stood at the edge of the bush, watching what was happening. Something was happening that she did not understand. I was lying immobile on my nearly complete roof for nearly ten minutes. I observed the first movements of the "cub" beginning its descent procedure. It descended for a few yards and stayed there for a few minutes, then repeated the feat a few more times, as if it were waiting for a maternal reaction.

When the cub reached the ground, the devoted mother uttered the characteristic guttural sound that seemed to command the cub to run into the woods. The mother bear galloped behind it. They both disappeared in seconds.

I went and cut another pine tree to provide enough bark to finish the roof. I removed the bark shells in the same way I had done before. I carried them up many times and finally at the end of the day the roof was finished.

A feeling of accomplishment that I never imagined possible swept over me. It was the opposite of the growing impatience felt when one gets nearer and nearer to a delayed completion.

The completion had a delicious taste. Honey, chocolate, and caramel all blended in sweet deliciousness.

My dreams on this night were of the same delicious experience.

Dance of the Bears

Diary Day 28

Northern Light Ballet and the Dance of the Bears

I had left the internal furniture for the final details. This day my hands would be making furniture. The bed was my first priority. It was made from a huge dry pine tree so that no pine resin or moisture would get on my sleeping bag or covers.

There was no soft mattress or any mosquito netting. The thin sleeping bag for a mattress and a jacket or other clothing was rolled up be used as a pillow.

The inside of the tent had a fine screen netting on the vent opening which serves both as ventilation and protection against insects. The tent had a door zipper closure. The cabin was not as insect proof as the tent. When inside the cottage mosquitoes had to be essentially kept out by keeping the door and the windows closed. The intruders that made it in succumbed to the smoke.

I also made a shelf to accommodate my stuff. Invariably clothes in a hunting camp end up hanging everywhere. They are rarely hanging in the most suitable place.

Arctic Adventure

This made me think about the fact that the extremely rustic camp environment and innumerable discomforts meant that only the most adventurous women would find it appealing. I on the other hand found it wonderful. I had the comfort of a cabin and I was about to add a shower that could be used indoors or outdoors.

Even so the shower would most comfortably be taken in the middle of the day. Water could be warmed and put into the portable shower tank.

Inside the cabin the shower was performed while standing on stones that drained the water to the outside.

Outside the shower was hung on a high tree branch.

In both cases the water was let out, bit by bit, so that a shower would only take about four to five gallons of water of water.

The bathroom was external and far from the lake. It was always a small hole dug into the ground. Once used it was immediately covered with dirt. This avoiding flies and bad odor.

The stove was always an improvisation. The pan hangs, by a wire on a wooden tripod, over the fire or hot coals or it is supported by a grate between two stones.

Barbecue is the easiest thing to prepare. A metal skewer or an improvised wooden limb serves to hold the meat over the hot coals or fire.

This gives a brief idea of the daily life inside the forest.

Only lovers of adventure and nature take pleasure in situations that lack the comfort of modernity. It is an extremely rewarding experience for those that love coexisting and experiencing the spirit of nature.

An enriching feeling of accomplishment passed through me when I finished the last piece of furniture. It was very gratifying to have done both a small and at the same time, a great achievement of building a strong and safe shelter and having done it all on my own.

At last night came. This was the first night I would be under a ceiling as comfortable as it was warm. I would use my kerosene lantern for the first time. From now on I would be spared from the weather and be in a perfect, safe, rainless environment.

I would be in a cabin that I erected with my own hands. I had the feeling of a winner. I had fulfilled a dream.

It was an achievement that fed my adventurous spirit.

I had achieved it in the context of an extreme environment. In the context of man lovingly embracing and holding nature sacred.

It could be said that this was a very pure place, isolated from the urban environment. This place had a musical vibrational range and pitch that truly seemed to lift the soul much closer to the one above.

It was one of my most beautiful and memorable nights.

I closed my diary as the day ended and the dark of night embraced the world around me.

I reactivate the campfire. I warmed some water and took my shower. The weariness and the cold made me almost fall asleep by the fire. The uncomfortable stool kept that from happening.

After a careful look around with the flashlight to make sure no beast was lurking around. I carried my rifle and went to the lake to fetch enough water to brush my teeth and have some at the side of my bed.

When I got to the lake to get the water, I saw them. The "northern lights" they were presenting their ballet!

I decided to take the canoe and paddle until I reached the middle of the lake. I lay down in the back of the canoe and watched the divine spectacle for hours on end.

Arctic Adventure

I fell asleep.

I awoke to a sound I had only heard twice before. Two bears were fighting. It came from the direction of the "Headdress" hill.

The cold I had felt when I awoke left me as I paddled the canoe there. With my flashlight I saw two male bears fighting over a female.

She was impassive in this quarrel. She was trying unsuccessfully from above to approach the hanging bags with the moose meat. Seeing her unsuccessful approach made me feel like a victor. I had successfully thought of a solution that I had never heard of before.

This single-minded bear focused on the smell of the meat was about to take a plunge from above. It circled and smelled the air in an attempt to identify perhaps another possibility of reaching what would be a feast. Probably countless other bears had tried unsuccessfully to reach the banquet.

I aimed the flashlight beam at where the bears were standing. They tried to catch the light.

The dispute ended when one took a tremendous hit and went rolling down the hill. He was bleeding and bruised by the sharp claws of the adversary. He ran into the forest.

These fights do not always end in death. The loser leaves, sometimes injured, but they usually heal and recover quickly.

Tireless northern lights accompanied my return to the camp.

I put more fuel into the fire and heated up a delicious hot chocolate.

I had returned with a good piece of meat for a banquet the next day.

I thought that the bears unable to eat the moose would have their appetite redoubled and might come to my camp. I expected that I would have bears visiting me during the night.

I retired to my cabin. I went to bed with my rifle at the ready.

I guessed right.

The bears made a huge mess, they triggered the "alarm", but I did not even hear it.

They did not bother me as I slept in the warmth of my cabin, my "hunting lodge."

Diary Day 29
A Floor, A Hammock, and Reading Comfort

They did nothing except tear a pair of trousers that I forgotten hanging out to dry. I found the rags it had become far from the camp.

The birds were happy. They sang at the top of their lungs, making the day happier. Under the beautiful blue sky and the pure mountain air, I transferred everything from outside to the inside of the cabin, now my official "hunting lodge."

There were only minor details to complete. At last, everything was almost done. It was a wonderful feeling that I never imagined possible. Doing it by myself made me more sensitive, more impatient, to getting the cabin completely done. The closer to completion the greater the anxiety and desire to get done.

The last light of our sun king dyed the horizon. He seemed to shy away from the great dark stellar mantle of the Arctic night.

The Arctic cold even in the spring is incredibly present at nighttime. It comes suddenly in a dizzying decline and only with the insistence of the sun on a new day does it slowly yield for a moment of mild temperature at the height of the day. I went inside to get a blanket. I took advantage of it and took my seasoned teapot that had twice faced the onslaught of the bears and went to prepare a hot chocolate at the fire.

Arctic Adventure

The fire dimly illuminated the cabin that was so unusual in this setting.

Sitting on a rustic but new bench, I sipped my "hot chocolate", watched the cabin, in my cloak and did not tire of observing the different realms that made this scene.

A moonless night, now without fire flames that no longer heated their embers, allowed me to see a unique, wonderful sky of which I could be a part as I never before had the opportunity.

What purity in a total absence of luminosity?

No noise, no movement except that of an owl that from time to time ventured a peep.

Now lying under a warm blanket to keep warm, I was toasted with a first metallic flash in the sky.

It was the "northern lights"!

A show where a harmonious ballet of lights surrounds the most unbelieving beings and invited me to a higher sphere of human feelings. It was the privilege of a few. It elevated and made one reassess the parameters and values of our lives.

It challenged many parameters of our insistent attempt to perpetuate our eternal insignificance. It challenged the human constructs of pharaonic works of self-projection or in the rotten political scenario.

It made the point that in fact, the greatest greatness is in the simplest acts and that we really need the courage,

To apologize and recognize when we make mistakes, or

To dedicate ourselves to a sick, troubled person.

Courage in the simple act of having patience with others and listening to them. A friendly word uttered at the right time, to someone who needs it, is of immeasurable value.

It was a moment eternal and unique, where my spirit was marked in an odd way. My body knew it was time to enter the world of dreams. It was already complaining about its well-deserved rest, because not having even used the clock for a day, it knew dawn was nearing. The best hours of my life had passed in one night.

I woke up in a mixture of infinite peace and a certain melancholy. Melancholy is what the ancient Romans called, "I do not know what."

I devoted myself to the preparations for another table and another bench. I was already prepared to provide more comfort to my brother and my friends for the next hunt. A rustic comfort of being able to sit at the table for a meal.

From a small roll of thin sheet metal, which I had to handled carefully not to wrinkle it with my hand, I mounted the duct that would carry the smoke and exhaust heat from a metal fireplace. The duct would radiate heat until the moment of its exit through the roof. The hood over the fire was also composed of the same material. It would have to be mounted near the height of the fire, so that it had the effect of diffusing the heat. This was an essential contraption to keep the whole room warm when the temperature was low. And it was always low, excluding some twenty days of summer when the maximum could reach eighty degrees during the day, falling at least to about forty degrees at night.

The bottom of the fire area in the cabin was a little worrisome. I made the floor around the fire area out of flat stones. It was a mosaic assembled one-by-one that I tried to make as flat as possible. I assembled the floor with flat stones, in an artisan work. The stone area accommodated the fireplace and firewood. I finished this area with a space to accommodate a hammock.

The rest of the cabin had a wooden floor. This was the area where I positioned the bed and the table.

I could read a good book by the light of a lamp at night or in the hammock by day.

Diary Day 30

Drink of the Gods

A quiet uneventful day passed. I focused on building the floor, sawing, nailing, hammering, and making the fireplace.

I waited to construct the most laborious part of the cabin. It was the stone floor. I knew the stones needed to be brought in as soon as possible. The clouds were warning me that rain would be coming soon. From the excessive heat of the day, I knew that another Arctic storm, never mild and always feared by nature, was possible.

I carried stones in until I thought there were enough. Then I set out to get some dry wood. Late afternoon was approaching, so I had to hurry because huge wind gusts warned that the renowned fierce weather was approaching this end of the world. I passed the strap of my rifle on my back, took the ax, and went to the "Bear Avenue" to gather dry wood.

Arctic Adventure

The best wood to find is that of a pine fallen by the wind, which has not reached the ground but is supported by another fallen tree. When the pinewood encounters the soil it will rot, but it will take years, to serve the natural cycle of enriching the stony Canadian soil.

Canada because of its climatic conditions, in its fields and woods, does not have many of the venomous, unpleasant animals and pests we have in Brazil. It does not have termites, scorpions, snakes, and spiders. They would not survive the Canadian cold. Given the conditions of its soil, were it not for the cold with all the snow and ice that accumulates annually through the harsh winter to melt in the spring and turn the continent into "half land half water", Canada would become a desert region. Particularly in the mountainous regions, the absence of land is glaring.

I entered the pine forest with the usual care. Since the place with the best wood was really the "Bear Avenue". It was where it looked as if the pines had fallen in a domino effect. There was much wood dried better than any man-made dewatering machine.

Already young pine trees were appearing in the middle of the fallen ones. Some reached almost two feet tall, suggesting a year or two of growth.

The pines that were felled and piled up would easily hide a bear walking on all four. I would not be able to see the movement. The quantity of "coconuts" identified this as the place of the forest warriors.

I walked a little more and saw what remained of a bear confrontation. There were bones scattered all over. I found the jaws, and I separated them. By the amount of tartar on the teeth, I guessed it to be the jaws of a rather very old adult. The two jaws would become an external decoration near the ridge of the cabin roof.

Standing forests, with vertical trees, provide a better environment to see a bear. Fallen trees like the ones in the "Bear Avenue" where there was no open view was very uncomfortable. I felt a shiver rise up my spine as I went to the place where the best dry wood was located. I had harvested all the wood for my camp on Headdress Lake from this spot. I was glad this was my last time to gather dry wood for my new cabin, my lodge, my "fort".

I never had any surprises while I was working with the chainsaw. It seemed to be a noise that hurt the bears' eardrums.

There had to be some relationship with this non-appearance of bears while the chainsaw was on. Nonetheless I always remained attentive.

The problem could be post-shutdown. I dragged the cut pine branches to the fire pit area on two trips.

Just for information, bears hibernate during winter in burrows and holes beneath rock formations where they shelter from the snow. Caves are very few, and I have never found one, thus proving the point. Most of the burrows are under fallen trees. The roots of large trees that have fallen leave a great crater and the possibility of shelter from the snow.

Knowing this, it made me double my attention when I frequented the "Bear Avenue". It had the largest concentration of bear dung that I have ever seen in my life. The "Bear Avenue" was a very large circulation area, and it seemed the dwelling for many of them. I came here several times, and it seemed that each time there were more and more "dung bombs" scattered on the floor.

I had a need for dry firewood. I needed to cut thick branches that yielded good, thick, long burning, firewood.

I only brought out thick branches and pine tips. And pine tips on a standing tree are more than 50 meters up. I was sure it would give vertigo to any young bear that climbed to its top.

Arctic Adventure

I quickly moved the gathered firewood into the cabin.

The weather was threatening to collapse the world at any moment.

My boat! I went to the lake to tie the canoe before the wind took it. I ran down to the lake, but I was too late. The wind had taken the canoe to the middle of the lake.

I had seen this movie before.

I felt myself marveling at the fury of the storm. The sound of distant thunder was drawing nearer now. One could see nature bow down before the storm.

On the land, from the youngest to the most grown pines, without exception bent over in respect.

In the water, the waves now spread drops of water into the wind that carried them away. Other drops from the sky came successively to meet them again and again.

I watched a true spectacle as the lightening rays raced on their journey to the highest point, a tall pine on the mountain nearest the camp and ran down the length to the ground!

I watched as the wind threw the canoe on some nearby stumps. I ran at once for my canoe as the first drops of heavy rain began to fall. I was able to guide it to shore as the wind changed towards the cabin. I tied it off well and then ran for the protection of the cabin and a place to dry off.

Moments later the wind brought the smell of smoke and fire.

The smoke became intense and an immediate concern the smoke. A forest fire presented the greatest fear. The smoke indicated that one was beginning.

I wondered what to do.

The wind was blowing toward the cabin. I knew there was a lake between the fire and me, but it could reach me by going around on the south bank.

I did not know what to do. What I could do was to save the rifle and ammunition, clothes, and supplies. I filled a plastic bag with the few clothes I had brought. I put the ammunition, matches, a pot and a frying pan, few supplies into my backpack. I wrapped my rifle, machete, hunting knife in plastic bags and sealed them with duct tape.

If I had to, I would take refuge in the middle of the lake. I was lucky to have a boat at hand. Looking out at the canoe, I saw it was banging on some stones. I did not think twice. I took off my boots because they were the last pair that I had. Then I went out into wind and rain and dragged the canoe up on the shore.

I had the silly thought that running out of underwear and boots would end any chance I had for romance.

I had my plan of escape ready.

Only God shuts down any type of forest fire.

I would stay out of the way but ready to escape.

As I watched its rising fury, I imagined it would soon reach the right and left sides of the lake. The fire moved fast as it was driven by the wind.

I have the habit of praying, and this time, yes, I prayed.

The fire fueled by the furious gale was taking on frightening proportions. But what was once a few thick raindrops, took on such intensity that I thought it might overpower the fire. That's when a flood flowing from the sky began. It was not a rain anymore, it was a waterfall coming from the skies, because I could not see my boat at twenty meters.

I got excited.

The wind in turn was very strong, but it did not topple the trees.

Arctic Adventure

The roof was properly tested and approved. The only leak was where the duct of the fireplace went through the roof. I had stuck stones between the chimney and the wood, afraid that it could catch fire from overheating.

In the comfort of the cabin, I stood for hours watching the storm slowly lose its strength.

I felt extremely happy and comfortable after finally seeing the forest fire completely exhausted and that my dream of having a hunting lodge in the Arctic remained in tack.

Lightning still streaked down from above, but it was more distant.

I thought, if the thunderbolts had fallen after the rain, all the forest would have been decimated by the flames.

I felt fulfilled, I began making plans for a future to bring my brother and friends to this paradise. A paradise full of emotions and achievements. A place where I felt closer to the Father. Where more than ever I was in his company. Where I more than ever talked with Him and felt the closest to Him. I felt Him as never before.

But today's adventures and emotions had reached the maximum level of adrenaline. The Arctic is delightfully wild. I appreciated the senses of the people who live here.

Today, deservedly, I will toast, in the sepulcher of this fireplace, and taste this "bottle of wine" drink of the gods, to having lived here!

If it were not for the calendar and diary that was filled with facts and narratives every day, I would not have the notion that the following day completed my thirty days of adventure. Time is always elusive. It had evaporated the past days and I felt tomorrow should only be day one, not day thirty.

I was happy on the one hand to the reunion with the family, but on the other hand I felt a melancholy longing as I considered the emotions of the great adventure that I had experienced.

Manfred Zepf

I was looking forward to an uncertain future.

Would I ever return to this paradise?

I then fell asleep to the patter of the rain.

I woke up with mixed emotions for in a few hours it would be my departure.

Diary Day 31

No Bill!

I grabbed the canoe and went to the "Headdress Hill" to retrieve the little meat that was left. I would give this to Bill.

Now it was up to my friend Bill with his Cessna. Would Bill come as scheduled?

I washed one of the meat sacks and hung it in the wind to dry.

I was already filled with longing. It gave me a bitter taste to leave all this behind. My return luggage that I did not want to prepare was insignificant. There was no charm in preparing the little that would return with me.

I felt uncomfortable leaving these days behind.

I ate the last of the delicious, dehydrated fruits. It was strange but their delicious flavor was for some reason missing.

I took a shower in the icy waters of the lake, which gave me an "up". I then very reluctantly collected, my fishing tackle, ax, hand saw, machete, cutlery, lamp, sleeping bag, boots, gloves, and chainsaw.

Arctic Adventure

I had used all the gas in the chainsaw cutting the green logs. The wood was piled up inside the cabin. The green pine wood gave the cabin a pleasant refreshing scent.

I arranged all the rest, the ropes, the nails, and the tools on a shelf next to the pine bed. I looked to the future when I would meet them again.

Pans and cooking utensils were all hung and fitted along the log walls.

Except the things Bill would take with him, I left everything else. I left my blankets. I hung up my washed, dried clothes as if I would wear them tomorrow.

I also left a few cans of peaches and powdered milk. I put the coffee, rice, and beans inside the empty metal cans of milk powder and left them as well. Although little, they were in cans that had passed the sneaky squirrel toughness test. It was not a lot, but it would be a relief to anyone who came here lost and hungry and looking for a safe haven.

I wrote a note and pinned it to the wall with my hunting knife. It said, "use whatever you need, save it and keep everything else as it might be useful to someone like you!"

At the door, I carved: the word "LIFT UP", with an arrow pointing to the gap.

I put away the rest of the fuel. I emptied the lantern, and everything else that winter could burst through arduous freezing cold.

I prepared a fire to guide my friend Bill's landing.

Then I prepared my coffee and sat down to enjoy my dehydrated fruit and the last ration of cookies.

I admired the odd beauty of the log rustic and magnificent cabin. It gave a pleasant balance to the idyllic beach of "Headdress lake."

The blue sky was clear with no clouds in sight. It was in the Brazilian language, "the sky of the Brigadier". There was no hint of a storm. A light breeze touched my face as my thoughts filled my mind, as I looked on the horizon. I knew that at any moment the sound of Bill's Cessna would break the golden silence of the moment.

We had agreed that he would leave Camsell Portage early in the morning. We should be skiing out on the Cessna's floats in this mirror of translucent water between nine and ten this morning.

Nine a.m. arrived. With growing anxiety, my heart beat a little louder.

Ten a.m. and no there was no Bill. I saw and heard nothing on the horizon.

By eleven, I reached a point of uncertainty. It was well past the agreed to time.

I checked my diary. Yes, today was the thirtieth day. I checked the days, date by date, again. I thought maybe I might have fooled myself.

I checked all the notes from the first day. I checked the days. I counted on the fingers of my hand. I had not made a mistake. It was the thirtieth day. It was thirty days since my arrival.

Today was when I was scheduled to return to civilization. I was divided between the happiness of the reunion with my family and friends, and the anticipated nostalgia for the time I had spent in this heaven in the North.

I had felt this longing yesterday.

Was it really a return to civilization?

The first wrinkles of concern made me pick up my diary and log in the time. It was now one in the afternoon as I wrote down what had happened.

I watched the hours go by: Two-o-clock, Three-o-clock, Four-o-clock, Five-o-clock.

If Bill came today, it would not be possible to return on the same day.

I wondered what had happened and I started to worry.

The sky was a clear blue. The weather was excellent.

The fact that Bill did not arrive was strange.

Every day in the late afternoon, before our star king threw its last rays and yielded to the robe of the deep night, dusk slowly creeped in.

The scene reinforced the huge unknown, and my uncertainty grew. My thoughts were many and conflicted.

What had happened to Bill?

Did Bill return safely to Camsell Portage, thirty days ago?

Arctic Adventure

On his way here, did he come to any harm?

I wondered how many hypotheses and questions I would think through.

In the evening I relit the fire. I had kept it burning with green pine branches and leaves between nine in the morning to three in the afternoon, so that Bill could easily locate me. I had provided a column of white smoke all day which could be seen from many miles away in that blue sky and green forest.

I set up the grille that had survived being handled by bears and by me. I barbecued a seasoned piece of moose meat. I took in the fact that it might not be the last barbecue that I would need to prepare.

After dinner, the night with its mantle of beautiful, endless distant stars dominated the land. The night, as it did on my second night at "Lake of the Headdress", seemed colder.

I relaxed myself with a late-night coffee and some dried fruit.

I leaned back. The light of my candle let me begin to reread the book that I had brought and which I would leave. Reading is my way to divert my thoughts and relax and get to sleep.

Sleep became a disrupted sleepless night. Two insistent, mischievous noisy bears came to the door and cried as if asking to come in.

A board knocked on the door causing a noise.

I got up and burst into loud crying at the door. I repeated it but the one at the door was not frightened. It fought with the other bear. They knocked some sticks out of the fire.

Through the crack I was able to watch everything. But what I wanted more was to frighten them away.

They gave no respite. They wanted to come in. They sniffed, smelled the door, and scratched at it because of the smell of the steak. After an hour, I threw the steak out on the ground.

They gave truce for few minutes and then they returned to the door.

As if it was not bad enough, they defecated everywhere giving off a soft, stinking rotten coconut smell.

The outside "smell bombs" seemed to reach through the walls and tried to grab me.

They did not find it easy to pick up a good evening meal. They had no fear of light, of the noises, whistles, and pounding of pots that I made. I've never seen such boldness.

They circled the bunker, they scratched insistently at the door for hours. Finally, they gave up.

I thought about the bear-proof construction. The cabin gave me the peace of mind that I was in a solid and protected hunting lodge, so necessary in these places.

It was almost dawn when I fell asleep of exhaustion.

"God Bless Canada."

Diary Day 32

God Save Canada

I was dreaming that I heard a distant roar of a plane approaching. I abruptly awoke when I heard water splashed by skis from a seaplane.

Yes, it was the sound of the Cessna. I was not a dream, it was Bill!

Yes, and I had my eyes open.

Before hurrying out to help Bill anchor the plane, I looked around the camp. There was no sign of the bears. There was just "shit". It was the most correct expression in the world for the coconut mess the bears had distributed at "Lake Headdress Camp".

I rushed to the lake's bank and took in the beautiful site of the plane gliding across the lake toward me.

With the engine off, Bill was approaching.

"Halloo Manfred," he called out! "Please help me stop the plane."

"Hold the rope," he shouted.

I tied the rope to the stumps in the lake.

"Hey!! My friend, what a beautiful cabin! I cannot believe it" he continued.

"Hi, Bill, did you intend to give me a heart attack," I asked?

"Why? Did I wake you up," he smiled and asked?

"I saw no sign of smoke to guide me in the landing. It was lucky that the wind was so calm wind so that I could circle the lake to land in this mirror of water," he continued.

"I saw no movement in the camp, I wondered if you had survived the bears," he said as he laughed.

When he told me, he had missed day thirty, it was enough for us to fall to the ground laughing.

"Only missed it by one day! Bill said as he grunted with shock from getting totally drenched by the icy water of the lake.

"How did your stay go," Bill asked as he walked up to the cabin and asked how he was to get in?

"I'll tell you the details on the return flight. I think you'll like the stories I have to tell," I replied as I demonstrated how to open the door.

"And that jaw fixed at the entrance to the cabin, how big was this bear? It was a giant, huh?" Bill continued.

"I'm not sure of the size, but I think it was huge," was my response.

"How do you not know the size," Bill said in a surprised tone?

"I do not know why because I did not kill any bear while I was here."

"No, that's impossible," he said.

"And this cabin, the size of these logs how did you manage to lift them? Where's the Bulldozer," Bill rambled on?

There was nothing I could say.

"The cabin!!! It's fantastic. "Impossible, Impossible," he finished in a quiet complement as he shook his head.

He took some pictures of the bunker. We had a coffee. He caste the fishing line three times and chose two beautiful specimens of northern pike to take home to his wife.

He then looked at me and asked "Manfred, where's the luggage?"

"I only have this bag with a change of clothes and personal hygiene, and my rifle. Everything else is yours, like the empty gasoline cans. One is almost full," I replied.

"What about the chainsaw? And will you leave all the rest as well," was the next question?

Yes, I answered.

He was reading the note that I had written that welcomed the next user.

"Yeah, you love it, otherwise you would not give it to anyone who might need it. That's the true spirit of the Canadian," Bill said as he looked over to me.

The next moment seemed to be the Cessna wings waving goodbye to the camp. The heading on the compass was 180 degrees due south.

I had tears in my eyes.

On the way back I massacred Bill my many stories

He had a few questions and I had long and enjoyable answers.

We were back to "Civilization" before we knew it.

I have never felt so loved.

"God save Canada!"

THE END

Manfredo Zepf

Epilogue

I have always had the habit of planning my travels and adventures in advance, because it is always difficult to be very far from Brazil, the country where I lived.

Our group of hunters had already scheduled a pronghorn and mule deer hunt in Wyoming, USA for the coming year. I was able to hunt a beautiful trophy next to Devils Tower. This was the first national monument named by President Teddy Roosevelt in 1906 and is part of Black Hills. This was the place where I had one of the most wonderful hunting experiences. My brother Conrado made a memorable "Mule Deer" barbecue at the foot of the Devils Tower. My friend Lairton made the famous Brazilian drink "caipirinha". It is usually made of cachaça, lemon and sugar and ice. Instead of the ice, he used the snow. The barbeque and the drink were memorable!

It was four years later that I went back to the cabin with my brother and two friends, Lairton and Paul for a week.

Arctic Adventure

Bill took us and stayed for the week. He did not want to hunt, but just to enjoy good times and indulge in fishing for the northern pike. It was exciting to take off with the same Cessna and fly on the compass, zero degrees or due North. Wanting to see paradise made me a little impatient. It took the same time as before but this time it seemed much farther.

Seeing the cabin from the air moved me. It was a delightful feeling. It looked exactly as I had seen it when I left.

Bill took the plane in to land on the mirror of the lake surface. A "silver" spray trailed as the plane floats touched the surface. It was a spectacular landing.

I was the first to jump in the water and hold the plane. The water was not "hot" at all, yes it was as cold foot numbing as it had been the last time.

I left the task of tying with Bill and the rest of the hunters and ran to the bunker. I took only my 30-06 Weatherby and my knife. The knife was the key and the secret to the opening of the door.

The message on the door was no longer legible. It had been scratched off by countless bear claws.

The Arctic has powerful weather. I checked the cabin for damage. It was exactly as before. By its climatic conditions, the Arctic does not have ants, termites or other insects that could damage the wood. And the cabin had no visit other than the insistent nail marks everywhere on the outside. The cabin had survived the onslaught of these beasts.

Conrado was delighted. He said would have liked to have participated in the construction of the cabin.

We unload the suitcases, rifles, and groceries. It was very nice to be reunited with everything I left from my last trip. I brought only a little more clothes and equipment to supplement what I needed.

The Inflatable canoe, it was in perfect shape and now the two oars would be used.

We prepared all the hunting equipment and as always, each one of us was on the alert and with their rifle on their backs.

My brother always worried about feeding his appetite had already picked up the fishing rod and on his first cast caught a Northern Pike. He boasted that he was a great fisherman. His joy infected Bill who cast his line with an artificial bait and in seconds caught a slightly larger one. This guaranteed a robust northern pike lunch.

It was moose hunting season. We planned to leave the next morning with the canoe. The goal was to select one with a trophy grade set of antlers. On the way of the flight in we saw some males with monstrous antlers. That's what everyone came for this time.

This first day was a day of reunion with my own bunker. And I basked in a day of admiration from my hunting companions.

We made a pleasing bonfire and sat around together talking, telling stories, and laughing a lot. The evening darkness delivered a wondrous star filled cloak across the entire sky.

It was a very pleasant evening. Bill warned us that thunderstorms were predicted for the next few days. We teased him saying that he knew the metrological information before we left and that he was taking advantage of it to say he was a "weather channel".

Next morning, Conrado and Bill headed toward the crest of the "Headdress ridge". My friend Paul and I headed to the opposite side where I had seen a beautiful elk. Paul was sweating and could no longer walk. He stopped in the shade to rest. He was startled and jumped up and his eyes were wide-eyed, asking me, "What was that?" I laughed, I explained that he was disturbing the mating ceremony of the partridges, which make a very loud and serious sound as they flap their wings against their breasts.

With no thought to moose hunting, Paul fired and retrieved what was left of the partridge after being shot with a Winchester 300.

We walked back to the camp. Paul had become a little more apprehensive because he now had a partridge that exuded a "food scent" for the bears.

Conrado and Bill heard the shot and decided to come back so they could help get the moose they thought we had shot down. They were laughing and teased

Paul about traveling so far to hunt a partridge. There was nothing left of the little fried partridge when lunch was over.

In the afternoon they all left for another hunt until dark. This time they were looking for anything!

On the third day the Conrado, Bill and Paul left in the canoe and arrived at the connection between the two lakes where they saw a moose with a calf.

My brother soon after realized his dream of shooting a moose. It had a handsome, but not so large set of antlers.

There was a pack of wolves close by.

As they removed the hide, they separated the meat and salted it. Paul brought in the canoe loaded with meat. I stored it inside the cabin.

It was not over yet. Bill and Conrado returned to the camp and brought only the skin of the head and the antler. They had left some ribs and pieces of meat. Bill saw danger in the fast-changing weather. He told us that he needed to get the plane out ahead of the ever-growing wind. He planned to safeguard the plane by flying around behind the storm to another lake. He planned to return before dark but if he could not, he would spend the night where he had landed. He pointed out that they had to safeguard the plane from the storm.

Conrado, who is also an airplane pilot, quickly gathered a bunch of snacks, water, and with his 30-06, the two left the lake as the wind got stronger and the thunderstorm intensified.

We hurried to get everything inside the cabin. We left only the well-tied canoe out on the lake. It was a chance for it to take advantage of the rain and get washed off.

It was a monstrous storm that hurled itself at the camp. Once again, I felt powerless before what came down from heaven. Paul got into bed and prayed. "Oh my God," he said, "I've never seen anything like this storm. I do not want to die yet. I still want to marry and have children, Oh my God!"

We laughed a lot at the end of the day when I told Bill and Conrado. They had flown around the storm and had seen gigantic cumulus nimbus clouds of an almost black color shooting out lightening across the entire expanse of forest.

"It was frightening to see the columns of water that poured from the clouds into the forest and the lakes," Conrado recounted.

Bill made the point that so much water at one time would have caused problems for the plane's moorings. It would not have been able to handle the fury.

These Artic storms purify the whole of nature. It strengthens the soul and gives it peace.

The burning bonfire made a difference as the cold became intense. Conrado, Paul and Larington had on the previous evening commented that the Arctic cold did not seem too bad.

Bill told everyone to look up at the sky. The firelight had kept us from seeing the weak but beautiful northern lights. They displayed faint variations of color. Sometimes the change was slow and then at other times it was very fast. We each wondered what these lights meant to the inhabitants of this place. We each gave our interpretation. We all agreed it was the creation of God.

Two of the sleepers opened an Artic sawmill. They snored so loud I was sure no bear would come close. The thermal sleeping bags ensured a warm night in the cold of the Arctic.

We woke up and went through the usual routine of peering through the cracks of the door, looking carefully around and then throwing a blanket a few meters in front of the door. If the blanket was not attacked, then we went out carefully and reconnoiter the area. This morning, surprise, bear feces! Three huge piles! Not even the snoring chased them away. No one heard the bears and they had nothing to destroy. I do not think they even made it to the bunker. It was probably because of the snoring. Who knows?

Arctic Adventure

Conrado and Lairton went to see about the carcass left on the edge of the lake. I believe that the mother moose should be thanking us today for distracting the wolves that were in the pursuit of her cub. The six wolves, all adults, were all at their moose banquet. They did not even bother about the strange creatures that came across the lake. For prudence Conrado and Lairton did not disembark but watched the ferocity and force of those jaws from the safety of the lake.

Crows rattled the nearby trees. Conrado and Lairton did not venture nearer. Surely, they would have like to have taken some meat, but the wolves had the priority. When wolves were in packs, not even the bears have entered this fight, because wolves are bold, fearless, and intelligent in attack.

I would like to understand the communication between them.

My brother came back early because he was assigned to cook the barbecue. He prepared his seasoning and began to prepare a delicious barbecue while I went to show the rest the team, the "Bear Avenue".

Bill stayed behind and kept Conrado company at the camp.

The saw dust from the dried and cut logs I made with the chainsaw were still present, somewhat darkened but not rotten. It had been four years! It was incredible.

Lairton and Paul, were impressed by the amount of scattered bear feces.

We walked along the side of the "Bear Avenue", because nobody dared to come close to the fallen trees. The bright sun beat down. but it made the forest next to the "Bear Avenue" seem black and impenetrable.

We agreed that at four in the afternoon we would take the bones of the moose that would be our lunch and place them in the "Bear Avenue" and we would wait for the approach of any bears between two nearby pines. Each one of us would be responsible for specific angle of view, out to about 50 meters. We were sure that the bones would attract a bear. Lairton and Paul left with a high "respect" for the place. They classified it as highly dangerous, with gigantic stools that meant the bears were marking it as their territory and in their way saying; "This is our house. Do not dare to come in!"

We had, a moose meat barbecue, roasted potatoes with parsley, capers, and butter. This was lunch in a refined restaurant, surrounded by a mother nature.

Wow how we ate.

We took a break and then prepared a bag of bones and leftovers from lunch. Then we walked cautiously, entering the dark forest of hundred-year-old pine trees to the dozens of fallen and broken trees in the "Bear Avenue". The bears had many hiding places under roots and trunks all the fallen trees.

Silence is the second-best weapon to have in hunting bear. The first is always your rifle.

We walked a few yards, stopped, and watched. We advanced but walked softly and stepped so we would not break any branches. The forest around is only of pines with no other plants or foliage. The soil is mostly old decomposing pine needles, branches, and mosses. The scenery is beautifully frightening.

Lairton whispered that it seemed impossible to miss seeing a bear. It took ten minutes or so to walk about twenty meters.

Paul pointed in the direction of the "Bear Avenue" and said he had seen a bear. Neither Lairton nor I could see anything, but we were alert as we looked at the end of the tree because it had a giant root that would easily give cover to a bear.

Paul immediately put the sack with the bones on the ground and we moved away from it. We proceeded in three measured moves to the two pines that we had previously chosen as the place we would stay during our hunt.

Later we would share the interesting fact that each of us felt like we were being watched. The bag must have been exuding a fantastic smell of Moose.

But fifty meters away it remained untouched.

I thought this was odd. Then after about half an hour of waiting, Lairton with his eyes wide open saw a far-away shadow. It was between some very distant pines on the opposite side of the "Bear Avenue."

It was a medium-sized bear that was circling the moose bag but staying a good distance away. It was going back and forth but it did not approach the bag. It was acting stealthily and staying behind trees. I figured there must be a larger bear somewhere about that made the smaller one so cautious. Very little time passed, before it rushed off. He ran desperately and he was looking at his pursuer.

None of us could see the bear that chased him away.

We all knew of the presence of an alpha male and the adrenaline immediately hit the thousand level mark. Five eternal minutes passed then we finally saw the alpha bear.

We had agreed that Lairton would shoot the bear. We would take a shot only if his shot were not fatal. The bear was walking slowly now, stopping and sniffing, for it knew of our presence. It was heading for the sack when it suddenly jumped and stopped near the pine root mentioned earlier. The bear had jumped off the fallen trunk as if it were nothing. What agility.

I looked to the rear as Paul and Lairton looked after the giant. As he walked toward the sack, he stopped and started looking at us. He lifted his snout, sniffed the air, and stopped again. He knew there was something near that was not a bear. He came a few meters toward us, sometimes sniffing at us, now sniffing toward the sack.

I again looked to the rear. If the alpha bear were there, I knew no other bear would dare challenge him. But I was not going to miss anything. The big bear stopped within fifty yards of where we were. He stopped and sniffed the remains of the moose. He looked at the bone and looked up at us as well. Thoughtful or cautious it turned in our direction.

Lairton brought his Weatherby Vanguard 30-06 up to his shoulder and shot the bear in the center of the head. It immediately fell to the ground.

We knew we would need to quickly leave the area. We had taken down the alpha bear, the Don of this territory. The other bears would move in quickly. We could not clean it here. We would take it to the camp.

I went for backup and called Bill and Conrad. My God, what a weight! We bound three small pines together. We did this twice and created a stretcher. We rolled the bear onto the stretcher and put a rope around it. It was necessary to do so because it diminished the drag of it to the ground. It took all of us working together to drag it back to camp. I kept one eye on the stretcher and one on the forest. We could not be neglectful. We were only half-way to the camp when we heard bears fighting over the bag of bones.

We were all sweating when we got to the camp. We lit the three campfires to discourage bears and began to skin the bear. As soon as we finished skinning and cutting up the meat, we put the remains of the bear in the middle of the camp between the three fires. I then stoked each fire with extra wood so that we would have light to see if the bears invaded the camp.

We prepared a tasty bear meat meal and enjoyed an evening of conversation and then a star-studded night.

Our hunting was done. The Cessna would take off with a maximum load.

The night was long! We took turns as sentinels. The bears were lurking all about. Two bears approached and were sharing the treasure of meat and bones. A third bear approached and fought with both. The fight went on for over an hour. The bears would run away from each other and jump over the fire to get away. They were quick and agile enough that they did not catch on fire. They ended up spreading bones all over the place.

We woke to the endless noise of the quarreling crows as they fought over the remains that the bears had abandoned.

We looked forward to two more days of fishing, eating moose, bear, and fish. Conrado and I planned to swim in the lake. Lairton, John, and Paul laughed and said they would take a pass at the swimming.

Lunch was of made up of bear ribs coated with barbeque sauce and seasoned with pepper. This would be accompanied with butter topped mashed potatoes. The desert was tangerines, and Ovaltine.

It was a great meal.

I did not know, nor did I imagine, that these moments in time would be the last moments that this group, of hunter friends, friends of adventure, a brotherhood that supported each other and enjoyed common and memorable moments of immense happiness, would spend together.

Arctic Adventure

We scheduled a trip for four years later to return and hunt together again to hunt for grizzly. The trip did not happen because Bill had to undergo emergency cancer surgery. For two more years he fought like a warrior. He underwent two more surgeries, but he lost the battle.

The journey to the cabin no longer had the charm and magic that it had in the past. The cabin was a symbol of dreams. It was a complete adventure and a joy to be shared with friends.

I have never gone back there!

Maybe someday?

I know the cabin is still standing.

I know...

About
Manfredo Zepf
Born in 1957, in Sao Paulo, Brazil

He was born in Brazil, on a farm, where until the age of seven he only spoke in German, he only learned Portuguese when he entered school.

At a young age, he won a pelt gun, and he and his brother, Conrado, competed to see who could kill more mice that were attacking his grandfather's corn stash.

At school because he had a German name and accent, he suffered the aftermath of the Second World War. He overcame the bullying and he learned to live with the taunts.

He lived in many cities and states in Brazil, like Guarujá, Santos, São Paulo, Itajaí and others until he was fifteen.

He won his first shotgun, a Spanish Sarrasqueta 16 gauge, that he still owns. With his Spanish shotgun, at the age of 15 he hunted his first animal, a Capybara. She weighed more than he did. He sweated getting her out of the swamp area, but he was happy.

He has hunted ever since.

Manfredo received a Bachelor of Administration from the Fatec Baixada Santista Rubens Lara University in 1982

He is now fluent in German, Brazilian Portuguese, Italian and has an intermediate knowledge in English, Spanish and French.

He got his airplane pilot license when he was 17 years old.

He was the manager of two FM radio stations in Brazil, from 1979-1981.

In 1982, with his brother Conrado, he established, a metallurgical business that had seven hundred fifty stockholders and ran it until 1998.

He became a sound engineer and established a sound and lighting company to support singers and bands all over Brazil.

He organized sound, stage, and lights for more than three thousand three hundred live concerts.

He created and held events such as,
- Febanita (Festa da Banana de Itanhaém), Rodeos,
- Salvador Summer Festival, Bahia in Brazil.
- Ilhéus Summer Festival Bahia, Brazil.
- Indian National Festival was a yearly event in Bertioga, Sao Paulo until 2008. It was considered the largest indigenous cultural event in the world.
- The financial sponsors for Manfredo's events were. Mercedes Benz, CEF, Sebrae, Honda, Yamaha, Volkswagen, Banco do Brasil, Johnson & Johnson, and others.

He became Secretary of Tourism and Commerce for the City of Bertioga from 2001 to 2008 and organized events of national and international scope.

He spoke at the UN in 2006 at the World Forum on Human Rights that focused on the Indigenous Peoples throughout the world.

He owned a disco and event house from 1979 to 1996.

In 2008 he went organic farming and became the owner of Santa Rita Farms and was focused on producing certificated organic fruits, vegetables, and greens, "Viva Mais Organicos", live more organically is its motto.

He and his family are all living in Miami.

Manfredo is married to Ana Rita, since 1993 (yes, I can't miss the date…my wife is always a challenge).

He has one daughter, Helga, 24, that has a Mechanical Engineering degree and is pursuing her PHD in Material Engineering at FIU.

He has one son Flávio, 22, in FNU, pursuing a Business Administration degree and playing on the FNU Soccer team.

He opened an Interstate Truck Transportation Company, as his new project and new challenge.

About the Editor - Translator
Ronald E. Mueller
remwriter95@gmail.com

    Ron grew up in what is now Flint River State Park in Southeast Iowa. The 170-year-old house Ron lived in is built into a hillside. It faces a 125-foot-high cliff towering over the little Flint River. The house and the land talked to him about the passing of time, the struggle to conquer the land, the struggles people faced and the wonder of nature.

    He climbed the cliffs, crawled into the caves, dove from the swimming rock, collected clams from the bottom of the pond, gigged and skinned frogs for their legs. He trapped muskrats for fur, hunted raccoon in the dead of night, and hunted rabbits in the dead of winter with only a stick. His young life was outdoors, and nature tested him. He walked to a one room stone schoolhouse uphill both ways. It was a great way to grow up.

    His experiences inter-twined with snippets of fantasy lend themselves to the adventures Taelo leads the reader through.

    Ron has told many similar stories to impart life values and influence the thinking of his children and now grandchildren. He feels stories are a wonderful means for parents and their children to engage in meaningful discussions about behavior and fundamental values and principles.

    The Arctic Adventure is a great true story that inspires and reinforces all these values.

Arctic Adventure

Appendix 1: International Travel Items List
Passport - (check validity of it and visas)
Old Passport - (if the valid visa is on it)
Driver's license
Credit Card (s)
World Health Card
Airfare etc. / loyalty cards
Dollars / Euros / traveler checks
2 Checkbooks $ / (per round)
Prod. Exit guides Foreigners
Shopping List / Orders / CD
Booklet Notes and Expenses
$ P Belt
Eye Patch to sleep
Inflatable Pillow
Cell phone / Alarm clock
Agenda (electronic)
Pens
Sunglasses
Eyeglasses
Maps
Scotch tape
Padlocks
Laptop (charger, Internet cable)
Headset (mic and earphone)
Web cam
Comics / Crosswords
Personal hygiene
Medicines
Pants
Shirts
Coats
Bermuda
Shirts
Socks
Briefs
Swimsuit
Hat
Hat
Video camera
Camcorder Charger
Camcorder Battery
Virgin Camcorder Tapes
Camera
Flash for Camera
Telephoto lens
Tripod
Memory card
Camcorder Cable X Laptop
Camera Cable X Laptop
Disc Man / Discs / MD
Destination people addresses
Mailing addresses
Slippers
Gloves

Empty suitcase for back
Umbrellas / disposable covers
Switchblade
Deck
Visit cards
Thermal bag
Thermos
Coffee

Appendix 2: Hunting Trip Add Items List

- Boots with respective lining
- Wool socks
- Shawl
- Beanies
- Hunting pants (thick)
- Hunting pants (thin)
- Coats
- Hooded cold weather pullover
- Earthworms
- Belt
- Wool Shirts
- Gloves
- Backpacks
- Raincoat
- Poncho
- Musketeer
- Screen hood against mosquitoes
- Knife
- Machete
- Small flashlight
- Large flashlight
- Crab or spotlight
- batteries
- Coarse salt
- Old mud
- Hunting license /
- Shotgun/rifle
- Bullets
- SFPC traffic guide
- Photos last hunt (for evidence ...)
- Latest trophies release guide
- Export guide for the hunted trophy
- License (s) of said animal (s)
- Rope thick
- Rope light
- Video (last) hunt
- Cushion for climbing plants
- Binoculars
- Waterproof match
- Candles
- Compass
- Clock
- Mug

Appendix 3: For the Arctic add listing

- Brimmed hat / cap
- Ski mask / scarf
- ski goggles for snowmobile
- boot cover
- gun case for snowmobile (soft)
- warm mittens
- Mittens, heather
- Thin insulated goose feather coat
- Sleeping bag -15 degrees Fahrenheit
- Gloves -15 degrees Fahrenheit
- Degrease camcorder
- Thermal protector for camcorder
- Thermal protector for ammunition

Arctic Adventure

Published by: Around the World Publishing, LLC

www.ingramcontent.com/pod-product-compliance
Lightning Source LLC
Chambersburg PA
CBHW081355070526
44583CB00020B/2559